Choosing from a Me

- **keyboard**   Press **Alt** and keep **Alt** down while pressing the underlined letter of the menu you want to display. **Alt+F** displays the File pull-down menu. Use arrow keys then to move through the menu's options. Press **Enter** to select a highlighted option.

- **mouse**   Point and click over a menu name to display that menu. Once it's displayed, click on whatever option you want.

- **access keys**   Many menu options have access keys that let you, with a single keystroke, select a menu option without having to display the menu first. For example, **F5** selects **Run**.

The Primary Math Operators

Operator	Description
+	Addition
-	Subtraction
*	Multiplication
/	Division

Online Help

When you get stuck, the **F1** key sends out an SOS.

alpha books

The Relational Operators

Operator	Description	Example
>	Greater than	If Amount > 40 Then
<	Less than	If userAge < 21 Then
>=	Greater than or equal to	If txtSales.Text >= 20000.00 Then
<=	Less than or equal to	If Balance <= 100.00 Then
=	Equal to	If button = 1 Then
<>	Not equal to	If Answer <> Correct Then

tear here

The Most Useful Buttons and What They Do

Button	Description
	Create new form
	Create new module
	Open existing project
	Save current project
	Display Main Design window
	Display Properties window
	Start application in design mode
	Stop program execution
	Stop execution, return to design mode
	Toggle breakpoint
	Display value in code window
	Display structure of calls
	Single-step code
	Execute next procedure or statement
	Pointer, selects items
	Picture Box, holds graphics
	Label, holds text
	Text Box, accepts user input
	Command Button, triggers actions
	Check Box offers multiple options
	Option Button, gives the user a choice of one option
	Combo Box, drops down a list of choices
	List Box, displays a complete list of choices
	Drive List Box, displays a disk selection
	Directory List Box, displays directories
	File List Box, displays filenames
	Shape Tool, draws squares and circles
	Line Tool, draws lines

The Complete IDIOT'S Guide to VISUAL BASIC 3

by Greg Perry

alpha books

A Division of Macmillan Computer Publishing
201 West 103rd Street, Indianapolis, Indiana 46290 USA

For my friend Larry Hoefling, the "Prevue Guide" man. The world knows your voice, but I know you best as a friend whom I don't see often enough.

©1994 Alpha Books

International Standard Book Number:1-56761-486-8
Library of Congress Catalog Card Number: 94-65311

96 95   8 7 6 5 4 3 2

Interpretation of the printing code: the rightmost number of the first series of numbers is the year of the book's printing; the rightmost number of the second series of numbers is the number of the book's printing. For example, a printing code of 95-2 shows that the second printing of the book occurred in 1995.

Screen reproductions in this book were created by means of the program Collage Plus from Inner Media, Inc., Hollis, NH.

Printed in the United States of America

Publisher
Marie Butler-Knight

Managing Editor
Elizabeth Keaffaber

Acquisitions Editor
Stacy Hiquet

Product Development Manager
Dean Miller

Production Editor
Kitty Wilson

Editor
Carolyn Linn

Cover Designer
Scott Cook

Designer
Barbara Webster

Illustrations
Steve Vanderbosch

Indexer
Rebecca Mayfield

Production Team
*Gary Adair, Brad Chinn, Kim Cofer, Meshell Dinn, Mark Enochs,
Stephanie Gregory, Jenny Kucera, Beth Rago, Marc Shecter, Kris Simmons,
Greg Simsic, Carol Stamile, Robert Wolf*

Contents at a Glance

Contents

Contents at a Glance

This page unintentionally left blank.

Contents

Acknowledgments

Thanks to all my pals at Alpha and Sams Publishing. Publishers shouldn't be allowed to have as much fun as you all seem to have when I see you.

This book's architect, Dean Miller, kept me inside the tracks. This book's commissioner, Stacy Hiquet, was doing mundane tasks while I worked hard; Stacy, next time you have a child, please plan it around my book schedules! This book's technician, Gary Farrar, takes things to the limit with accuracy and knowledge; Gee, Gary, I'm busy writing, and here you want me to be *accurate* as well? This book's Seinfeld consultant (every book should have one), Jordan Gold, kept me from being late despite his adherence to "Not that there's anything *wrong* with that!" attitude.

The others who worked on this book, namely Kitty Wilson and Carolyn Linn, have my heartfelt thanks because I just gave you the words and you turned them into non-mush.

As always, my family stands behind me so I don't stumble. Jayne, *mia moglie bella*, and two parents, Glen and Bettye Perry, instill something in me, but they haven't quite figured out what it is yet.

Recycling tip:
Tear out this page and photocopy it.

About the Author

Greg Perry is a speaker and writer in both the programming and applications sides of computing. He is known for bringing programming topics down to the beginner's level. Perry has been a programmer and trainer for the past 17 years. He received his first degree in computer science, and then he received a master's degree in corporate finance. Besides writing, he consults and lectures across the country, including at the acclaimed Software Development programming conferences. Perry is the author of more than 25 other computer books, including *Absolute Beginner's Guide to Programming, Turbo C++ Programming 101, Moving from C to C++, QBasic Programming 101, Teach Yourself Object-Oriented Programming with Turbo C++,* and *Teach Yourself Object-Oriented Programming with Visual C++* (all published by Sams Publishing). In addition, he has published articles in several publications such as *Software Development, Access Advisor, PC World, Data Training,* and *Inside First Publisher.* In his spare time, he lectures on traveling in Italy, which is his second-favorite place to be.

Special bonus: virtual text page.
(There's virtually no text on it.)

Introduction

You're Not Really an Idiot!

Despite its title, *this* book won't treat you like you're an idiot. Nevertheless, we all know that computers often make us *feel* as though we're idiots! This book is your pal; together, we'll laugh at Visual Basic, praise Visual Basic when deserved, and cringe when Visual Basic requires that we do something really idiotic to perform a simple task. (Fortunately, those times are few and far between.)

Who This Book Is For

If you've used Windows, a lot or a little, you're ready for this book! This book assumes that you can at least *recognize* a computer, find the keyboard, and insert a diskette. This book also assumes that you've used a computer and Windows, even if you've only played Windows Solitaire. If you've used Windows, you've used a mouse, answered Windows-like message boxes, and selected from menus. You don't have to be an expert! With patience, you'll be an expert soon enough.

You may be tired of seeing your friends get programming jobs while you're left out in the cold. Maybe you'd like to write some nifty Windows programs but just don't have the time or energy to go to night classes. Your old, worn-out computer could be in need of a hot programming language to spice up its circuits. If so, this book is just what the doctor ordered! Perhaps you've never written a computer program in your life, or you failed miserably if you tried. You'll find that this book finally turns the tide for you.

Why Do You Need This Book?

Despite all the press, Visual Basic cannot always be picked up intuitively by someone who's never programmed. Furthermore, Visual Basic is not always picked up intuitively by those people who program solely in the

DOS world but who want to move to Windows programming. Visual Basic is, however, light years ahead of many of the other programming languages on the market. In a way, Visual Basic is a programming toolkit with some easy features for beginning and expert programmers.

The Complete Idiot's Guide to Visual Basic 3 isn't like many programming books—it talks to you at your level without talking down to you. This book is like your best friend is sitting next to you, teaching you Visual Basic. *The Complete Idiot's Guide to Visual Basic 3* attempts to *express* without *impressing*. It talks to you in plain language, not in "computerese." The short chapters, figures, and occasional humorous straight talk guide you through the maze of Visual Basic programming in a faster, friendlier, and easier way than any other book available today.

What Makes This Book Different?

You don't have to know a lot about Visual Basic or programming to create simple, usable, and powerful Visual Basic programs. There are lots of books out there that try to make you an expert. That expert status does not, however, come from books; the expert status comes only from using Visual Basic.

This book gets you started with *using* Visual Basic. There are tons of technical nerdy things left out. Why? *Because you don't need them to get started with Visual Basic!* Why not learn enough to get started, and then, on your own, you can explore Visual Basic's nooks and crannies? We're not piloting airplanes here, for gosh sakes! Learn enough to know what's possible, and play around.

This book takes you from knowing nothing about Visual Basic to feeling comfortable with the program. More than that, this book makes you *want* to go to the keyboard and play with Visual Basic because you won't be burdened with all sorts of advanced *every-year-or-two-you'll-need-this-cryptic-option* fluff that you simply do not need.

What's in the Book?

This book contains 30 chapters, and it is broken into 6 parts. Within each chapter the book follows certain conventions to present information in a clear manner.

Any keys you need to press are in bolder type, like this: Type the letters **ABC** and press **Enter**. Sometimes, you need to press two keys at once, and they are given with a plus sign between them, like this: **Ctrl+C** means to hold the **Ctrl** key and press **C**, and then release both keys.

Throughout the book, a number of special elements are used to help speed the learning process and make this book even easier to read:

Background technical information that you should read only if you are interested. Not necessary for learning how to use Visual Basic.

Plain definitions of computer terms. Learn these and you too can "Speak Like a Geek!"

Generally worthless but occasionally helpful comments from me.

Tips on the easiest and fastest ways to perform a task.

Warnings and solutions to common problems.

Put It to Work
Safe ways to practice what you learn.

What Do I Do Now?

Turn the page and learn Visual Basic.

Trademarks

All terms mentioned in this book that are known to be trademarks or service marks are listed below. In addition, terms suspected of being trademarks or service marks have been appropriately capitalized. Alpha Books cannot attest to the accuracy of this information. Use of a term in this book should not be regarded as affecting the validity of any trademark or service mark.

Visual Basic is a trademark of Microsoft Corporation.

Microsoft Windows is a registered trademark of Microsoft Corporation.

Part I
Visual Basic's Basics

Visual Basic is the easiest way to create computer programs. Perhaps you've used a spreadsheet or word processor. You may have even used a computerized checkbook program. Perhaps you like to play computer games. Whatever.

When you want your computer to do something, you've got to find a program that does it. You can buy a program or write one yourself.

No matter how many programs are out there, there's always going to be something you want your computer to do that nobody's written a program to do exactly the way you want it done. Maybe you want your checkbook program to pay a few extra dollars in taxes every year, over and above what you actually owe (yeah, sure). People have too many different and unique needs for computer companies to think of everything that everybody needs.

That's why Visual Basic is such a great thing. When you can't find exactly what you need, use Visual Basic to create exactly what you need! Visual Basic creates Windows programs, with you, faster than any other program-writing system on the market.

Before you jump headlong into Visual Basic, s-l-o-w d-o-w-n! You're first going to get six helpful chapters that will eliminate some pain when you really go to work on creating your next best-selling program.

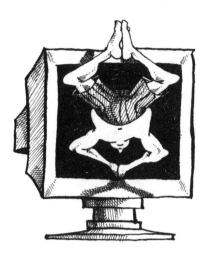

Chapter 1
The Bottom Line: Visual Basic's Really Vital Stuff

Remember the old *80/20 rule*? Economists, executives, and engineers love the 80/20 rule. It goes like this: "80 percent of the time, people only use 20 percent of a product's capabilities." There are all sorts of variations. Change the name to 90/10, 95/5, 75/25, or whatever pair of numbers add to 100 so the rule sounds best for the point you're trying to make.

Visual Basic programming has its own version of the 80/20 rule. It goes like this: "80 percent of the time, Visual Basic programmers use only 20 percent of Visual Basic's features." I got this rule's definition from a reliable written source. (I wrote it down, and then I read what I wrote.)

Let's cut to the chase. No Visual Basic programmer uses *all* of Visual Basic's power. In reality, there are just a few things that all Visual Basic programmers really need to know to be productive. Here's a list of those 10 most important things that every Visual Basic programmer must master:

1. Starting Visual Basic.

2. Arranging the Visual Basic screen to your liking so you're most productive.

3. Creating a new Visual Basic application from scratch.

4. Understanding *forms*, which are your programs' windows and the glue that holds your programs together.

Application is computer lingo for programs that you and others write.

TECHNO NERD TEACHES...

Programmers think it's cool to call Visual Basic *VB*. That's why I'll use *VB* a lot in this book.

5. Using VB's online help system so you don't have to keep those thick Visual Basic manuals lying all over your desk. (They'd only get in the way of this book!)

6. Using many of the *tools* of Visual Basic. When you want a specific tool, you'll use your mouse to pull one off the Toolbox, kind of like lifting a tool from a carpenter's toolbox. The tools produce the final application's controls.

SPEAK LIKE A GEEK

By the way, the *users* are people who use the programs. See, not every computer term requires an advanced degree in Geek.

7. Understanding and using graphical controls. *Controls* control your program (good name, huh?) and give your users neat things like buttons, dials, and data-entry boxes on the screen so the users can direct the program and type answers to your program's questions.

8. Familiarizing yourself with the Visual Basic *code* underneath forms and controls.

TECHNO NERD TEACHES...

Code is a bunch of close-but-not-English Visual Basic commands that you sometimes type.

9. Learning that Visual Basic includes many built-in functions that save you time and programming effort by supplying you ready-made code modules that perform mathematic and data manipulations.

10. Changing control property values, both during the program's creation and (via code) when the program executes.

Chapter 2
What's It All About, Microsoft?

In This Chapter

- Why Microsoft made Visual Basic
- The reason for Visual Basic's popularity
- What Visual Basic is
- What Visual Basic isn't
- Steps needed to produce results

You've just gotten a copy of Visual Basic, so you're ready to create the next best-selling Windows spreadsheet, database, word processing, and check-book manager program, right? That's ambitious, and your ambitions are to be admired. Just slow down a little, though. Visual Basic is the easiest way to create custom Windows applications, but Visual Basic requires some time investment before you can be productive. This chapter attempts to give you an overall feel for what Visual Basic can do, and why you should even bother with Visual Basic.

Microsoft's Visual Basic Aim

Microsoft, the company that produces Visual Basic, positioned the Visual Basic product in a unique way. In the mid-1980s, most computer *experts* (those are computer people who *never* feel like idiots, and so, therefore, they are idiots many times) said that the BASIC programming language was dead. BASIC was the forerunner of both Visual Basic and QBasic, which is now supplied with MS-DOS. Since the 1950s, BASIC was the language that all beginning programmers were told to learn first so they would be ready for a *real* programming language such as FORTRAN.

BASIC is an acronym that stands for *Beginner's All-Purpose Symbolic Instruction Code.*

In the late 1980s, C, C++, Pascal, and the other programming languages were dominating programmers' toolkits. The industry pundits said that soon even beginners would use Pascal or C in place of the old standby BASIC. BASIC had accomplished its original goal of giving programming to beginners, and now the industry had to grow up—and those beginners had to grow with the industry.

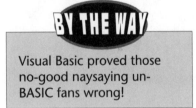

Visual Basic proved those no-good naysaying un-BASIC fans wrong!

In the early 1990s, Visual Basic took the reins of PC language leadership almost overnight! There might be more C and C++ programmers out there than there are Visual Basic programmers, but the Visual Basic programmers produce finished Windows applications faster than the speed of light compared to those who use other languages.

Why Is Visual Basic Popular?

Visual Basic contains the same BASIC-like language that beginners have relied on for years. Microsoft improved the original BASIC over the years. Visual Basic's programming language is just as easy as QBasic, but it adds all the extensions needed to produce Windows programs.

Windows programs are difficult to write. For everybody. Real programmers who use C and C++ (those people who produce Windows applications slower than the forward speed of a train going *backwards*) say that if you want efficient and flexible Windows programs, you cannot use Visual Basic. They have a point (see the section titled "What Visual Basic Isn't" later in this chapter).

What those real programmers almost always fail to tell you is that many of them use Visual Basic *first* to produce complete, working Windows prototype applications, then go to their C and C++ programs and spend tons of time producing the same Windows programs the hard way.

Visual Basic enables you to design, rework, produce, test, and implement complete working Windows programs, and you have *fun* while doing so. (The *visual* in *Visual Basic* comes from the fact that you move visual elements on the screen to design VB programs.) You've never had *so much fun* with a mouse and keyboard as you'll have with Visual Basic!

A *prototype* is a working model of something. C and C++ programmers create prototypes in Visual Basic before using C and C++.

What Can I Do with Visual Basic?

Basically, VB enables you to produce eye-catching graphical Windows programs. You perform most of that program development by pointing, dragging, and clicking with your mouse! As mentioned in the previous section, you produce these programs in fractions of the time it takes using other programming methods.

Don't worry about difficult-sounding terms you read about in the VB manuals, such as MDI, OLE, DDE, and DLLs. Some day you'll master them, but for now you can safely put them on the back burner.

In today's world, non-Windows DOS-based text programs are generally boring. The primary disadvantage of such programs is that you must learn a new command set for each program you use. Visual Basic maintains the application consistency Windows programs are famous for. If you've used a Windows program before, you'll probably be able to generate programs with Visual Basic.

Consider the program shown in Figure 2.1. On the screen are lots of Windows controls, a menu bar across the top, a standard window, and a mouse cursor. This figure shows a loan calculation application that comes with Visual Basic; it's stored in a file named LOAN.MAK. You'll learn how to load and run such applications in Chapter 5, "Controlling Visual Basic."

Some examples of Windows controls are *command buttons*, *scroll bars*, and *dialog boxes*.

Figure 2.1

A sample Visual Basic Windows application.

What Visual Basic Isn't

Visual Basic is not the most efficient programming platform in the world. Part of the problem is that Windows itself isn't the most efficient system, even on the fastest computers. When you run Windows, there's a lot going on under the hood. Windows is like a thick layer of protection between you and your computer; although that layer adds tools and safety, you lose some flexibility and speed over DOS-only environments. (Windows resides in memory along with DOS.)

This chapter has taken several shots at C and C++ programmers who create Windows programs. Now, it's time to pay the piper! Those C and C++ Windows programs run like lightning compared to equivalent VB programs. (Remember that VB is an abbreviation for Visual Basic.) Well, I don't want you to think that VB is *terribly* slow, but it's significantly slower than a program written in C or C++.

Visual Basic is not a true *compiler* like C and C++ are. Compilers generate faster and more efficient code than do noncompiled languages such as VB.

Visual Basic is not *entirely* for beginners. There are certainly some aspects of VB that are, honestly, not all that easy to learn. You won't hear about those aspects here! This book doesn't ignore them because they are difficult; rather, you simply don't have to know every aspect of VB to be productive with VB. After you know the fundamentals, and after you have played around with developing your own VB applications, you'll think the "hard" aspects of VB aren't hard at all.

Visual Basic isn't entirely visual! You cannot do *everything* possible in VB with just the mouse and VB's graphical tools. There are times when you'll have to suck in your gut and type instructions in the Visual Basic language. Of all the programming languages, though, the VB language is one of the easiest.

What It Takes to Be Productive

Here are the steps almost every Visual Basic programmer goes through to produce Visual Basic applications:

The instructions that make up a VB program are called *code*. The words *code*, *application*, *program*, and *instructions* are often used interchangeably. (The programming community likes to keep outsiders from thinking this business is easy to master.)

1. Decide what program to create in Visual Basic. This seems obvious! You must, however, decide what you want your finished product to look like. Along the way, you might change your mind as you develop the program, and VB makes making these changes easier than do most programming languages.

2. Use tools supplied with Visual Basic to plan the look of your program. You'll use the mouse and keyboard to design all the screen elements, text, and data-entry boxes.

3. Add whatever code your program needs to tie the screen's parts together, and add any customized details that can only be finished by writing VB language instructions.

A computer *bug* is a mistake that you or somebody else puts into a program.

4. Test the program thoroughly. When you have it working completely, and after you get all the bugs out, give it to someone else (a *user*) to test. Sure enough, they'll find bugs you never dreamed of. Fix all the bugs and design flaws that you missed the first time around.

That's it. The more you learn about VB, the more ideas you'll gain about what VB can do.

The Least You Need to Know

You've got the initial introduction out of the way now. Isn't it time you started using Visual Basic? Check out the following review list:

- ☛ Microsoft designed Visual Basic to give easy access for those who want to write Windows programs without a lot of fuss.

- ☛ Visual Basic enables you to create Windows programs in a fraction of the time it takes with other programming products.

- ☛ Visual Basic is visual; much of VB programming requires little more than moving elements on the screen with your mouse.

- ☛ Visual Basic does not produce the most efficient Windows programs, but don't let that stop you from creating all your Windows applications with VB.

- ☛ You'll have to learn the VB language and write some code with it.

Chapter 3

Revving Up Visual Basic

In This Chapter

- Learn about those pictures on so many Windows screens
- Start Visual Basic
- Exit Visual Basic
- Troubleshoot if Visual Basic doesn't start

Visual Basic can do little until you start it, or run it (*start* and *run* mean the same thing in computer lingo). Earlier in the book, you promised that you've used Windows before (you *did* promise, didn't you?). You must start Windows before starting Visual Basic. When you've got Windows up and running, Visual Basic is just a click away.

Launching Visual Basic

The *Program Manager* is what most people see when they start Windows. Figure 3.1 shows one such Windows Program Manager screen. The Program Manager holds lots of pictures called *icons*.

OOPS!

Your Program Manager might have more or fewer icons than the one pictured in Figure 3.1. Also, more icons might be expanded (*opened*) like the one in the lower-right portion of the screen.

Icons are like graphical menus. Icons enable you to start
related programs by clicking with the mouse.

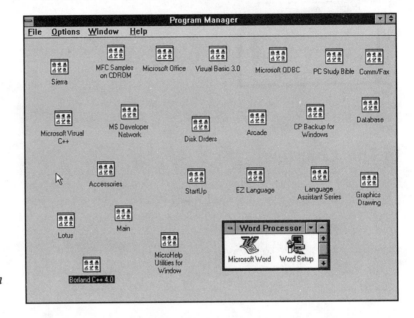

Figure 3.1

*A Windows Program
Manager screen.*

Figure 3.2 shows a *program group* icon. When you double-click the
mouse cursor over a program group icon, the program group opens to a
window like the one shown in the lower-right portion of Figure 3.1.

Figure 3.2

A program group icon.

Locate the program group icon labeled **Visual Basic 3.0**. Double-click the icon, and the program group opens, showing a wide range of colorful Visual Basic icons, as shown in Figure 3.3.

Program group icons look like miniature windows. Other kinds of icons take the look of almost anything.

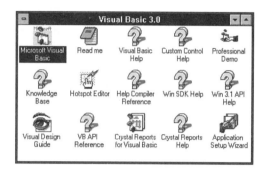

Figure 3.3

The open Visual Basic program group.

Even if you use Version 3.0 of Visual Basic, you may not see an exact reproduction of Figure 3.3's open program group on your own screen. That's okay. You may not have the Professional Edition of Visual Basic, so you'll have a few fewer icons. Don't feel slighted! The Standard Edition includes all you'll need for a long time, and this book covers only those features found in the Standard Edition.

The highlighted icon, **Microsoft Visual Basic**, is the icon you click to start Visual Basic. (Finally!) Double-click this icon, and Visual Basic begins. When VB finishes going through its start-up exercises, you see a screen that looks something like the one in Figure 3.4.

You might have an older version of Visual Basic. If you do, I *strongly* urge you to upgrade to Version 3.0 because of the advanced features and easier interface that Microsoft added to Version 3.0. When you first start VB, you see a message box telling you the version number of your copy of Visual Basic.

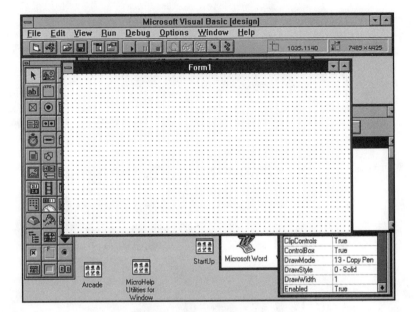

Figure 3.4

The opening Visual Basic screen.

TECHNO NERD TEACHES...

Visual Basic consists of lots of windows. In the next chapter, you'll learn a little about how to understand, place, and organize all those windows so you can manage them better.

In the lower-middle portion of the screen, notice that some of the Program Manager's icons show through some of Visual Basic's windows. In the next chapter you'll learn how to resize the Visual Basic windows to hide the Program Manager.

Jot down a note on one of those little yellow sticky slips that reminds you what to do before you start Visual Basic the next time. Here's what it should say: "Before starting VB, select **M**inimize On Use from the **O**ptions menu of the Program Manager's menu bar." After thus selecting from the menu, the Program Manager will shrink to a single icon and be more out of the way the next time you start Visual Basic.

Doesn't Work?

If you can't find the Visual Basic program group icon, you may have to close some Program Manager windows that are open. The open windows may be covering up Visual Basic's program group icon. (One icon in the open Visual Basic program group contains a highlighted title—the one labeled **Microsoft Visual Basic**. The highlight is a clue that you'll choose this icon the most often.)

If you still can't locate the Visual Basic program group icon, Visual Basic might not be installed on your computer. That's a bummer. You'll have to rely on the "Setting Up" section of your manual, or better yet, find someone to help if you've never installed software before. Luckily, Windows and Visual Basic do most of the installation work without needing your intervention.

If you found Visual Basic's program group icon, but you cannot seem to expand the icon into the Visual Basic window, you may have to adjust the speed of your mouse's double-click. Double-click faster, and if that doesn't work, double-click more slowly.

Figure 3.4 contains the opening screen for the Professional Edition. If you have the Standard Edition, you'll see *most* of the screen elements shown in Figure 3.4.

To close a Windows open program group window, if you ever want to, just double-click on the *control menu button*, which is the little gray button in the window's upper-left corner.

Get Me Out of Here!

Sure, you're just *dying* to do something with all those Visual Basic windows on your screen, but take just a moment to learn one important skill: *putting away* Visual Basic when you're done.

If your double-click still doesn't work, make sure your mouse cursor rests directly over the program group icon or the icon's title.

To exit Visual Basic and return to Windows, select Exit from the File menu at the top of the Visual Basic screen. This is how you exit virtually every Windows program. If you make any changes whatsoever to the VB application before you exit (even changing the size of a window, as you'll learn to do in Chapter 4, "The Screen's Too Busy!"), VB will ask if you want to save your changes and give you a chance to store important work before returning to Windows. Never turn off your computer with Visual Basic showing on your screen. Always exit Visual Basic and any other Windows program you might be running. Then exit Windows. Once you return to a DOS prompt, wait a few seconds more, and then you can safely turn off the computer. If you don't follow all these steps, you could lose valuable data.

The Least You Need to Know

You can now start and stop Visual Basic! Sure, the screen looks busy once you get VB started, but in the next chapter, you'll learn how to arrange the screen to suit your liking. Here are some key points to remember:

☞ Find the Visual Basic Program Manager group in your Windows opening screen.

☞ Open the Visual Basic Program Manager group by double-clicking the icon.

☞ Start VB by double-clicking the Visual Basic icon.

☞ Exit Visual Basic, and return to Windows by selecting Exit from the File menu on VB's menu bar.

Chapter 4
The Screen's Too Busy!

In This Chapter

- ☞ Learn Visual Basic's primary screen windows
- ☞ Resize (enlarge *and* shrink) windows
- ☞ Uncover hidden windows

This is the first of two chapters that show you how to manage your Visual Basic screen and menus. It's difficult to work at a messy desk, so clean your Visual Basic desktop before working with Visual Basic. (If you could see the author's desktop right now, you'd wonder why he doesn't practice what he preaches about clean desks!)

If you work a lot with Windows, you only have to skim this and the next chapter. Managing and navigating Visual Basic screens requires common Windows skills.

VB Anatomy 101 (or Identifying Screen Parts)

The rest of this book explains how you use things on your Visual Basic screen, so you might as well get some common terms down right now. Start Visual Basic now so you can try some things.

Be warned that there is more on your VB screen than first appears. Depending on your version and edition of Visual Basic (and depending on what someone may have done with your Visual Basic before you started it...), some of your VB windows might be covered up by others.

There are five common windows that make up the Visual Basic environment. (Actually, there are more, but these five are the ones you'll see most often.) Figure 4.1 shows the five windows, and labels important parts of those windows. Again, you may or may not see all of them on your screen now.

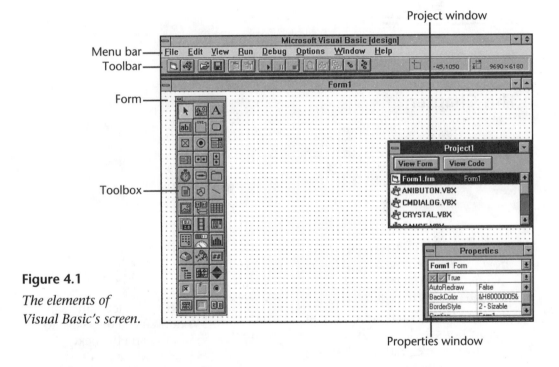

Figure 4.1

The elements of Visual Basic's screen.

Organizing the Screen

You may not see all the elements shown in Figure 4.1. This section gives you some advice on how to arrange your Visual Basic screen to make it more comfortable for you.

Consider the screen shown in Figure 4.2. Lots of the environment is covered up with other windows. Also, you can see the Program Manager peeking through the bottom. A few mouse clicks and movements produce the screen shown in Figure 4.1, where everything is neatly arranged.

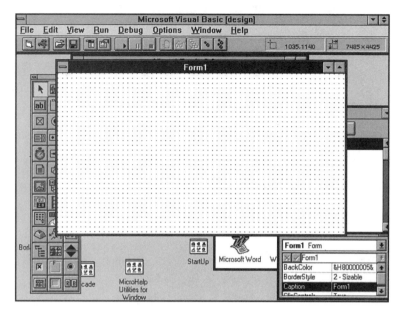

Figure 4.2

A screen needing arranging.

Grow a Window

Perhaps the best thing to do is expand the Form window. You'll learn later that the Form window is where you do most of your work. Therefore, a larger work area will benefit you. Point to the bottom edge of the Form window, and the mouse cursor changes to a double-pointing arrow. When you see this cursor, click and hold the mouse button, and drag the lower edge of the window down to the bottom of your screen before letting go of the mouse button.

In a like manner, drag the right edge (leave the left alone for now) of the Form window so that you've expanded the Form window to cover all of the screen, except for the top window that holds the menu bar and the toolbox. Your screen should look something like the one in Figure 4.3.

BY THE WAY

You don't have to rearrange Visual Basic windows when you start VB. Through menus and the mouse, you can get to any and all windows when you need them—you never have to see them all at once, but the next section describes how to see them all at once just so you can practice your window rearranging.

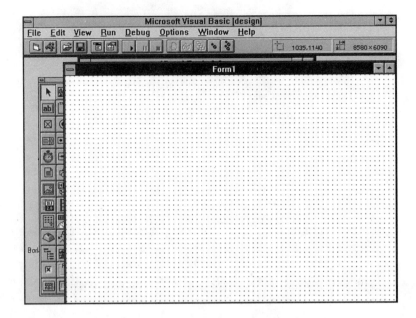

Figure 4.3

The resized Form window.

Sure, the Form window covers up other windows, but you'll uncover those next.

You can use this click-and-drag technique to expand or shrink almost any window you ever see in any Windows program. See how mastering one Windows program helps you master all the others?

Undercover No More

Despite the fact that the Form window is hiding other windows, the Project window and the Properties window are still there, underneath, waiting for your next command. Use the menu bar's **Window** menu option to uncover the other windows.

Display the **Windows** menu. As you can see, to display the Properties window, you can choose Properties or press the **F4** speedkey without choosing from the menu. Select Properties, and you'll see the Properties window.

Display the Project window by selecting Project from the **W**indow menu. If you ever hide the toolbox, no problem; to unhide it, simply select **T**oolbox from the **W**indow menu. Your screen now displays all the windows so you see everything.

There are other windows that you'll learn about later, such as the code window.

What's nice is that you'll *want* some of these windows to be covered much of the time so you don't have to show each of them every time you start VB. As you learn more about Visual Basic, you'll know when to uncover a window and when to leave one alone. You simply don't always need to see the Properties window, for instance.

Move Windows Out of the Way

If a window is in your way, you can move it. Click and hold the mouse button while pointing to the title bar of any window on your screen. The title bar is the top edge of a window, even when no title is actually there.

Try moving the toolbox by clicking its thin title bar (with no title) and dragging the toolbox to the right and left to see how easily you can place the window where you want it.

You'll often want to work on one area of the form, and keep the toolbox off to the side, still visible. You now know how to drag the toolbox to where you want it.

If Your Windows Overlap...

Sometimes, you'll end up with two or more windows showing on the screen, but not *all* of one of the windows is visible because another is covering it up. Figure 4.4 shows a toolbox partially hidden by a Properties window.

A mouse click is all you need to unhide a window.

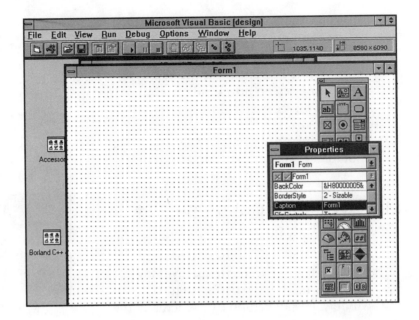

Figure 4.4

A partially hidden toolbox.

It's possible to close your Form window by double-clicking its control button in the upper-left corner. If you close the Form window, there isn't a menu option to get the Form window back on the screen. You must first display the Project window (via the **W**indow menu), and then click the View Form button at the top of the Project window.

If you need a tool from the part of the toolbox that's covered, you'll want to display the entire toolbox. (Use your imagination here! "Needing a tool" means that you want to click one of the buttons on the toolbox.) To bring a hidden or partially hidden window into full view, click the window's title bar. If you were to click the toolbox's title bar in Figure 4.4, the toolbox would completely show and partially hide the Properties window.

The Least You Need to Know

Now that you can move and resize the windows, you'll be able to get to the things you need when you need them. The next chapter continues where this chapter leaves off by describing other areas of VB's screen. Keep in mind the following:

☞ Identify the menu bar, toolbar, toolbox, and these: the Properties window and the Project window.

☞ Move windows around on your screen by dragging a window's title bar with the mouse.

☞ Resize a window by dragging an edge of the window.

☞ Display and hide windows by double-clicking the control button and overwriting one window with another.

This page unintentionally left blank.

Chapter 5

Controlling Visual Basic

In This Chapter

- Learn about Visual Basic's forms and project files
- Familiarize yourself with Visual Basic's menus
- Learn about the toolbar

This is the second chapter that describes navigating through the maze of the Visual Basic screen and menus. It sometimes seems as if Microsoft put *so many* helpful features in Visual Basic that the features often get in the way of each other. Also, the helpful and obvious icons on the toolbar aren't always that helpful *or* obvious to VB newcomers. Therefore, this chapter takes some of the difficulty out of using the screen's tools.

The Menus

Many of the VB menu options are just like the ones you've used in other Windows programs. You can use any of the following to choose a menu option:

- **The keyboard** Press **Alt** and keep **Alt** down while pressing the underlined letter of the menu you want to display. **Alt+F** displays the File pull-down menu. The arrow keys then move you through the menu's options, and **Enter** selects an option that you've highlighted.

A form is the background of your VB application. The previous chapter showed you how to resize the form in your Form window. Some applications might have several forms. Stay put... you'll see.

A *project* is a collection of VB routines, screen controls, forms, code, and everything else that makes up a Visual Basic application.

☞ **The mouse**   Point and click over a menu name to display that menu. Once it is displayed, click whatever option you want performed.

☞ **Access keys**   As you'll see shortly, many menu options have access keys that enable you, with a single keystroke, to select a menu option without having to display the menu first. Shortcut keys are often called *accelerator keys*.

The File menu is where you load and save your VB applications from and to the disk drive.

When you develop a VB application, you first begin by opening a new project. Well, actually, VB opens a default project named PROJECT1.MAK when you first begin. After modifying that PROJECT1.MAK project, you can save your work under the name PROJECT1.MAK or, better yet, under a project name you make up.

The File menu enables you to create new projects from scratch, save projects, and load (or *open*, in Windows lingo) projects that you've already created but want to work with again. If you create a project and later decide you want to add or remove a new control or form to the project, use the Add File, Remove File, and Save File menu options.

There are some other File menu commands, but the rest aren't important for you to know now.

The Edit menu enables you to do all the standard text-editing functions, such as cutting, pasting, finding, and replacing text in your VB programs. Perhaps the most important Edit option is Undo, which enables you to redo your last edit, whether that edit was a deletion, insertion, replacement, or even a format change of some kind.

The View menu enables you to see some areas of your VB application, such as the VB instruction code that's often hidden until you're ready to see it.

TECHNO NERD TEACHES...

If you want to distribute your completed applications, select the Make EXE File menu option, and VB creates a stand-alone Windows program that runs without the complete VB environment.

The **Run** menu gives you the tools for running the VB programs you create. Most of the time, you choose **Start** from the **Run** menu (**F5** is the access key) to see the results of your labor.

You won't need the **Debug** menu. You'll never make any programming mistakes.

Let's replay that one more time! Everybody makes programming mistakes, but we won't tell anyone about yours. When your program doesn't do exactly what it should, and there are no obvious errors, the **Debug** menu helps you find those obscure errors.

The **Options** menu enables you to modify the way Visual Basic behaves. This book explores some of the **Options** menu choices as you need them. For now, don't worry about changing any of the Visual Basic option settings.

Some menu options are grayed out. Those are not available at the time you display the menu. However, when you need to use those options, they will be available.

Almost every major Windows application has a **Window** menu, but you'll probably use VB's **Window** menu more than any other program's. By its very nature, as you saw in the previous chapter, Visual Basic's screen is full of win-dows, both hidden and in view. **Window** helps you easily manage those windows.

Use Visual Basic to create *end-user applications*. Users then can use the applications you develop.

The **Help** menu is virtually identical to most other Windows applications' Help menus. Nevertheless, programming systems such as Visual Basic require an online help system with a little different personality from those help systems of end-user application programs such as Word for Windows and Lotus 1-2-3 for Windows. Chapter 6, "I Need Help!!!" explores the **Help** system in detail.

All the toolbar commands are available from the menu. Depending on the strength of your mouse and keyboard skills, you might find that it's easier to use the menus than to position the mouse on top of a toolbar button. Using the toolbar is a matter of style and personal choice.

That's All I Need???

At this point, you might be saying to yourself, *"This* is all I need?...I've read a description of menu options, and I still don't know the first thing about what it really takes to create a VB application!" That's a good point. By going through the menus now, and the toolbar in a moment, you'll know more about what's available as you develop programs within Visual Basic.

Don't memorize all these options, as you'll only waste your time. Get the gist of the menus now. This book always tells you what menu option you need when you're ready for one.

Put It to Work

Select **Toolbar** from the **View** menu. The toolbar goes away! If you rarely use the toolbar, you might want to hide it so you have more screen space. Selecting **Toolbar** from the **View** menu puts it right back if you change your mind.

The Toolbar

Figure 5.1 shows the toolbar with its tools (the square buttons) labeled. Some of these tools are used in special circumstances. For example, the last five are for debugging sessions if you need help finding a programming error.

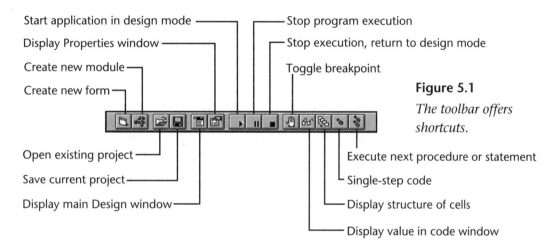

Start application in design mode ——————— Stop program execution

Display Properties window ——————— Stop execution, return to design mode

Create new module —— Toggle breakpoint

Create new form ——

Figure 5.1

The toolbar offers shortcuts.

Open existing project ——————— Execute next procedure or statement

Save current project ——————— Single-step code

Display main Design window —— Display structure of cells

Display value in code window

Why is there a toolbar? Microsoft attempts to give you push-button access to many menu commands. When you want to open an existing project, you can use a menu or you can simply click the mouse on the third toolbar button and do the same thing.

There won't be any more time spent on the toolbar. You've now seen it, and you know what it's for. As you progress with Visual Basic, you can come back to Figure 5.1 and recognize the uses of other toolbar buttons.

This book often reminds you when can push a toolbar button.

The Least You Need to Know

You are now acquainted with Visual Basic's screen. Although you don't necessarily know how to use all the menus and toolbar buttons and windows, you should feel more at home with seeing everything labeled and explained. Here are a few things you should remember:

- ☞ A form comprises the background of your VB application.

- ☞ A project file holds your application's forms, controls, code, and all related elements.

- ☞ You can select from the menus using the keyboard, the mouse, or access keys.

- ☞ You can learn the various menus by displaying each of the pull-down menus.

- ☞ The toolbar exists so that you can grab (with the mouse) controls when your application needs them.

- ☞ You can get rid of the toolbar if you want more screen real estate by double-clicking its control button.

Chapter 6
I Need Help!!!

In This Chapter

- ☛ Go through the online tutorial for a VB overview
- ☛ Press **F1** to get context-sensitive help
- ☛ Use the Help Contents to launch many helpful features
- ☛ Learn to navigate back and forth inside VB's help system
- ☛ Get help on any VB programming language command

Sometimes it seems as if we can't get enough help! (It seems as if there's *never* a manual around when you need one...) Visual Basic includes a comprehensive online help system. If you've used Windows help before, you should still skim this chapter, because Visual Basic's help system is honed for a programming environment, and there are a few special considerations that you don't always need in other Windows end-user applications.

Online means on the disk and ready for you to call up at any time.

An Electronic Tutorial

Visual Basic can help you learn Visual Basic (but not as well as *this book*). The Help menu contains an option called Learning Microsoft Visual Basic. When you select this option, VB displays the following lesson topics from which you can point and choose:

- ☞ Instructions
- ☞ How Visual Basic Works
- ☞ Creating an Application
- ☞ Writing Event-Driven Programs
- ☞ Working with Forms and Controls
- ☞ Adding Menus
- ☞ Debugging Your Application
- ☞ Using Color and Graphics

VB students have sometimes left this tutorial with more questions than answers. Many topics simply aren't explained in the detail needed for a true *tutorial*. The electronic tutorial, however, does give you an overview of Visual Basic, and each topic takes only a few minutes to read through.

F1: Visual Basic's 911 Phone Call

The **F1** key is the universally accepted Windows help key. No matter what you're doing in Visual Basic, pressing the **F1** key displays a Help screen related to what you're doing at the time. VB looks at what you're currently doing and displays help on that topic. This help awareness is called *context-sensitive help*.

Put It to Work

Here's an example of an **F1** action. Display any pull-down menu, such as the **File** menu (remember to press **Alt+F**, or click **File** with the mouse). Visual Basic displays the Help screen shown in Figure 6.1.

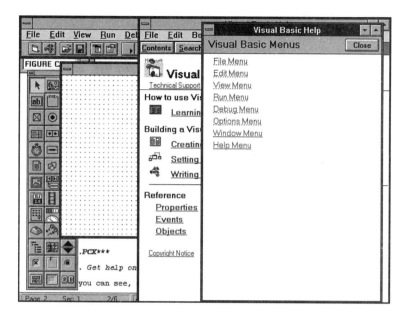

Figure 6.1

Get help on the menus.

As you can see, the help is topic specific. The help is titled **Visual Basic Menus**, and each menu topic is listed.

Run your mouse over the help topics listed. Notice that some green topics are underlined with dots, and others with straight lines. A green dotted underline means that you can go to another help topic screen simply by clicking that dotted-underline topic. If you want help on the File menu topic, for example, move the cursor over the words *File menu*. The mouse cursor changes to a hand (Visual Basic, it's not nice to point!) shape. Click the mouse, and you see a new list of help topics that coincide with each File menu option.

Any time a help topic is listed in green, you can get more information on that topic by double-clicking the topic with the mouse. The green topics are called *cross-reference* topics.

Click one of *these* choices (see, the online help system is just like a book in which you can flip to and fro to find information you want), and VB displays a Help screen about that menu topic. For example, clicking New Form gives you the Help screen shown in Figure 6.2.

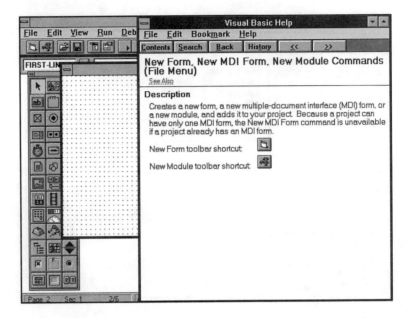

Figure 6.2

Help on the New Form option of the File menu.

Navigating Around

The Help screens, such as the one in Figure 6.2, all contain common menu and toolbar options. The Contents toolbar button takes you to the highest level of online help menus that exists. The Contents screen works a lot like a book's title page and table of contents. You can see at a glance the contents of the help system shown in Figure 6.3. One of the most important parts of the Help Contents screen is the Programming Language reference, which is discussed in the final section of this chapter.

To get rid of the Help screens, you can always select Exit from the Help window's File menu.

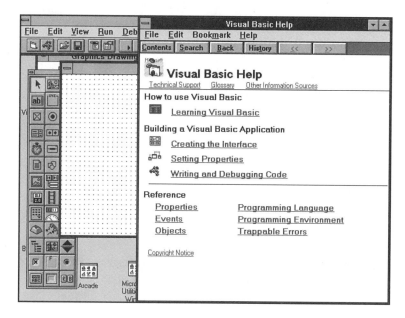

Figure 6.3

Viewing help's contents.

The Search toolbar button always displays the help system's Search window, as shown in Figure 6.4. You can scroll through the list of keywords looking for a specific help topic. If you type the first few letters in the help topic you're looking for, such as **vari** for help on the topic *variable*, you see a list of variable-related help topics from which you can choose.

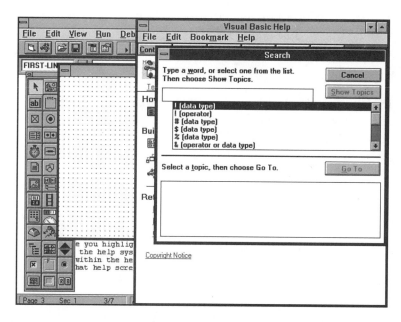

Figure 6.4

Searching for an online topic.

The File menu enables you to print any and all of the help topics.

Once you find and highlight a topic you've searched for, click Show Topics, and the help system displays a summary of every online topic available within the help system. Highlight the one you want, and VB displays that help screen.

The Back toolbar button takes you back through the help topic screens that you've looked at in the current help session. In a similar review manner, the History command button displays a scrollable list of help topics you've looked through; instead of sequentially stepping back through the topics as the Back button does, you can jump directly to *any* Help screen you've read during the current session.

The << and >> buttons work just like the rewind and forward buttons on a tape recorder. They walk you through the Help screens that come before (<<) and after (>>) the screen you're viewing. The screen that VB takes you to with << and >> aren't necessarily related to your current Help screen; they simply follow in natural order within the help system of topics.

The Bookmark menu option enables you to attach your own name (your *bookmark*) to the current Help screen. As you define new bookmarks, VB adds your bookmarks to the bottom of the Bookmark pull-down menu in a list from which you can choose.

The Help menu gives you online help about online help! Is all this too much?! It used to be that people complained that computers were too difficult to use. Now, help systems are so involved, it seems as if computers try to help *too* much.

Clicking the Help menu's Always on Top... menu option keeps the Help screen visible on your screen while you work with VB. (You can resize the on-top Help box so it's out of the way but still visible.) When you don't want the Help screen anymore, again select Always on Top... from the Help menu.

Visual Basic Helpful Stuff

Syntax is a language's spelling and grammar rules.

You've got to keep in mind that Visual Basic is not *just* a program that helps you move graphics around on a form (although that's a *big part* of Visual Basic, unlike other programming languages). Visual Basic is a complete programming language with a command syntax, and the online help system provides you lots of help that you'll use as you hone your VB programming language skills.

The help's Contents window contains the jump-off point for the online language reference. You'll find the Programming Language cross-reference topics on the Contents screen. Clicking Programming Language gives you the look-up window shown at the right in Figure 6.5.

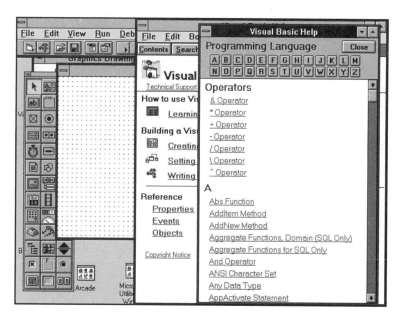

Figure 6.5

Look up any VB language word.

Simply click any of the letters at the top of the screen, and you see all the VB language's words that begin with that letter. Click any of the cross-referenced words that appear, and you see a Help screen on that topic. If the Help screen requires more than one screen length, use the scroll bars to bring more of the window's text into view.

The Contents screen gives you other important jump-off points, such as Events, Properties, and Trappable Errors. These are really advanced. Scan them now if you want—you'll understand them later.

The Least You Need to Know

F1 displays the context-sensitive help, but Visual Basic provides a lot more help than that. Cross-referenced words give you instant access to other topics related to whatever you're getting help on currently. The Help toolbar and menu commands give you the ability to navigate throughout the help system. Finally, the Help Contents screen provides access to the Programming Language help topics, the most important set of Help screens when you begin writing VB code. Here are the basic points to remember:

- ☞ Online help gives you instant (okay, *instant* relative to the speed of your computer and disk drive) access to Visual Basic's helpful advice.

- ☞ The **F1** key gives you context-sensitive help as you work in Visual Basic.

- ☞ You can search for any help topics. Don't yet know what to search for? You will soon.

- ☞ As you learn the VB programming language, you can get help on any of the language's words through the Programming Topics cross-reference on the Help Contents screen.

Part II
So, When Can I *Do* Something?

Too many times, newcomers to Visual Basic, with little or no prior programming experience, jump right into Visual Basic. They quickly learn that despite all its promises, Visual Basic takes a little orientation.

Congratulations! You've made it through the VB orientation class! If you now feel as if you know a lot but still know nothing, you're right on target. (That's the way the author always feels.)

You can now start Visual Basic. You can get help when you want it. You are comfortable with the menus. You know what Visual Basic is for. You aren't scared by all the windows when you start Visual Basic.

Despite all your knowledge, you cannot yet create a simple Visual Basic program! Don't fret, you will be able to, starting in the next chapter.

It's time to jump into the Visual Basic ocean. Hey, the water's warm. You'll have fun, and you'll see that programming with Visual Basic is often a snap!

Chapter 7
Your First Application

In This Chapter

☞ Finally, you get to create a real Visual Basic program!

☞ Finally, you get to *run* the program you create!

☞ Finally, you see how much you don't yet know!

You just *had* to have those first few chapters of introduction. When and if you get stuck, you'll be able to get help. Now you know what I'm talking about when I say, "Look at the Form window." If you're like me, though, you're itching to produce something really neat, something like a complete working Windows program with buttons, a menu, and all that cool stuff. Before you're done with this chapter, you will have built your first complete Windows application, and it'll only take a few keystrokes!

Poof! From Nothing to Finished Program

Start Visual Basic if it's not already started. You should be looking at a blank form with a toolbox, the Properties window, and the Project window underneath the Form window.

As you start VB, you'll notice a lot of *.VBX filenames appearing in the Project window. (Professional Edition owners see more than do Standard Edition owners.) A .VBX file holds special controls that you access from the toolbox.

When a builder builds an office building, the builder pours a concrete foundation. The Form window acts like a concrete foundation for your Windows applications. The Form window is the backdrop on which you place all of your program's controls, text, and data-entry boxes. The form is blank when you first create an application, and you fill it in by moving selected toolbox tools to the form and making those tools work together with code and settings in the Properties window.

Whew! It's a lot to absorb, but the previous paragraph explains just about everything you need to know now about Visual Basic. Don't worry, you'll see that paragraph in action as you progress through this and the rest of the chapters.

Some Common Tools

You're about to use some tools from the toolbox, so here's a short time-out to learn 4 of the most common ones. Depending on your edition, your toolbox will have either 23 or 39 tools. (The extra 16 aren't critical now, and you won't need the extended tools of the Professional Edition for a long time, if ever.)

When you become a Visual Basic guru, you might even add your own controls to the toolbox. The toolbox is not limited to the 39 tools of the Professional Edition.

Figure 7.1 shows the toolbox. Just like a box of tools, the toolbox sits around on your screen, waiting for you to select and use tools. A few of the tools you'll need first are labeled on Figure 7.1. You'll find that once you master these four basic tools, you'll easily understand and be able to use the others.

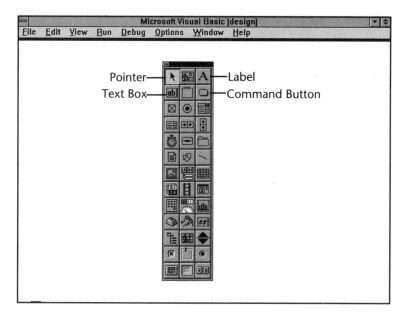

Figure 7.1

The toolbox, with the most common tools labeled.

The pointer is not really a control. When you click the mouse over the pointer, VB knows that you want to use the mouse for something *other* that selecting a tool. However, when you move the mouse over another tool (okay, *control*) and select that control by clicking, VB knows that you've selected that control and want to use that control in your application. For example, if your application needs a label, you double-click the Label control (don't do this yet; wait for the next section).

Table 7.1 contains a description of the controls labeled in Figure 7.1. Later in this book, you'll learn additional controls. For now, let's not go too far too fast.

Unlike a real toolbox, there is a virtually unlimited number of tools in VB's toolbox. You can select and place the same tool in your VB application 25 times if you need to.

For some reason, Microsoft insists on calling the toolbox items *controls*. Much of the time, this book does also, just to make Microsoft happy. Why, therefore, didn't they call the thing in Figure 7.1 a *controlbox*?

Table 7.1   Common Controls in the Toolbox, and Their Descriptions

Control	Description
Pointer	A non-control that lets you use your mouse for things *other* than using toolbox controls. In other words, if you've been using another control, such as the Text Box control, that Text Box control remains highlighted (in use) until you click the Pointer control or finish placing the text box on the form.
Label	A control that displays your text on the screen.
Text Box	Both a keyboard-entry capture box and a text display box. Unlike with the Label control, your user can see text and enter new text in a Text Box control.
Command Button	An on-screen Windows push button, with text that you put on the button, that the user can push (click with the mouse) to specify actions wanted in the program.

Don't confuse the *toolbox* with the *toolbar*. See Chapter 5, "Controlling Visual Basic," if you need a review of the toolbar.

Selecting and Placing a Control

This first application will be simple. You'll simply create a Windows application that contains a push button in the center of the window. (Remember, in VB and Windows terminology, on-screen push buttons are called *command buttons*, and that's what I'll call them from now on.)

To begin, you'll have to place a Command Button control in the center of the Form window. Remember, whatever you put (or draw) on the form appears in your finished program's window. You don't have to expand the form, because the smaller size that VB initially gives the Form window is ample for this first program.

Here are the two ways to select and place a control on the form (don't do either yet, just read through the ways):

☞ Click the control that you want to place on your form. VB highlights the control. Move the mouse to the Form window, where the mouse cursor becomes a crosshair (two lines forming a cross). When the crosshair is positioned on the Form window where you want the control, click and drag the mouse until you size the control to the size you want it (as you drag, the corner of the control expands or shrinks depending on your mouse dragging). When you let up on the mouse button, VB sizes and places the control the way you requested it.

☞ Double-click the control. VB places the control in the center of the Form window for you, and gives the control a good size. You then can move and resize the control if you'd like.

Which method appears easiest? The second one, of course, and that's what we'll use now. (Chapter 8, "Adding Pizzazz," shows how to use the first method of control selection.)

Finishing Your First Program

How can you *finish* the program if you haven't started writing it yet? You really have begun, because you started Visual Basic. A few mouse clicks and keystrokes, and you'll be done.

1. Double-click the Command Button tool. Visual Basic displays a command button in the center of the Form window, as shown in Figure 7.2.

Put It to Work

Walk through these steps one by one, and you'll see a VB application appear before your eyes!

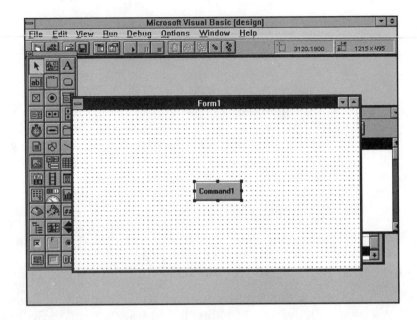

Figure 7.2

The Form window, with a command button.

The eight little black squares around the command button are called *resizing handles.*

See the eight resizing handles around the command button? If you want to, you can drag any of these handles to resize the command button (but don't do it right now).

2. As soon as VB places the command button on your screen, like the one in Figure 7.2, type **Hi!**. You don't have to press **Enter** after typing the word. The Properties window appears, but don't worry about it now.

You're done! You've just *written* your first VB application. Do you know that it would have taken a C or C++ programmer about 100 lines of tedious code to do the same thing?

All you have to do now is tell VB that you're done.

Running Your Program

You learned in Chapter 5 that the **Run** menu gives you the ability to run programs that you've written. Now that you've written a program, select **Start** from the **Run** menu.

As soon as you start the program, VB moves some of its windows off the screen to make room for your program. Figure 7.3 shows what your program looks like when you run it. Click the **Hi!** command button, and you see it press down as if it were a real button that you pushed on a control panel.

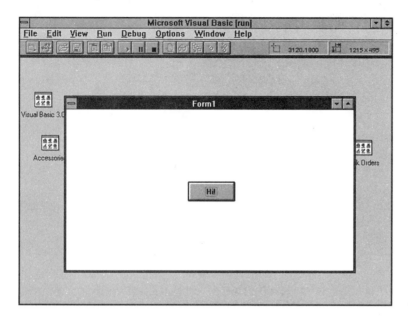

Figure 7.3
Your completed application.

Not Impressed?

Hopefully, you're not disappointed by your results. That's a great start for someone who's never programmed before. Look at the running program, and you'll see all sorts of things there. For instance, you can move the mouse to any edge of the window to resize the window. You can click the upper-right resizing button on the window (or double-click the title bar) to expand the window to full screen (click the same button to put the window back to normal size).

Click your window's command menu button (upper-left corner of the window), and a Control menu appears, like the one shown in Figure 7.4. This is a typical Windows command window; it is like those found in most Windows applications.

You can press the **F5** access key instead of selecting **S**tart from the **R**un menu.

The window initially consumes the same amount of screen real estate as did the Form window when you created the application. If you resize the Form window before you run a program, the resulting program's window will be a different size as well.

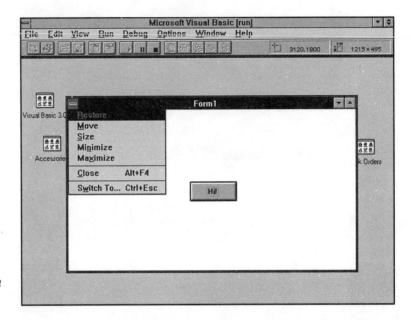

Figure 7.4

Your application even has a Control menu.

Visual Basic did a lot of background work to create this complete Windows application, and you only had to guide the process a bit and tell VB what you wanted inside the window.

In your applications, you'll want to supply a more elegant way to exit the program. That's what you'll learn in Chapter 8.

Get Me Out of Here!

Ready to quit the application and return to the Visual Basic environment? For now, you must display the Control menu (Figure 7.4), and choose Close. **Alt+F4** is the access key to selecting Close.

Save Your Work

In case you want to quit for a while before moving to Chapter 8, save your work. Remember that your application's form, controls, and all related files form a single project file.

Before saving the project, think for a moment about the form you just created. Although this is a simple form, you might imagine putting all sorts of controls on the form and linking them together (via code) to form complete applications. When you create a form, you can use that form in another application. Therefore, you must save both the form *and* the entire project.

The following steps save your form and project under project files named FIRST.FRM and FIRST.MAK, respectively:

1. Select Save Project from the File menu. Visual Basic displays a File Save As dialog box.

2. Although VB suggests you name the form FORM1.FRM, use FIRST.FRM. You don't have to type the .FRM extension.

3. When VB displays the Save Project As dialog box, enter FIRST.MAK for the project name. VB supplies the .MAK extension if you don't type it.

You can exit Visual Basic if you want, by selecting Exit from the File menu.

The MAK project file extension comes from the name *makefile*, a VB programming term for a collection of all the program and support files that form an application.

The Least You Need to Know

You are now a Visual Basic programmer! Honest! You guided VB through the program design, creation, and running process, and you witnessed the output from the program: a full-blown Windows application with all the common resizing and Control menu elements found in most Windows programs. There's a lot more to learn, and you'll modify your first application, learn a lot along the way, and have more fun than a programmer is supposed to have, in Chapter 8. For now, keep in mind the following:

☞ The toolbox contains controls that you'll use in your applications.

☞ Double-clicking a control is the easiest way to put that control in your application.

☞ After you create your program, run it by pressing the **F5** access key (which selects **S**tart from the **R**un menu).

☞ **Alt+F4** selects **C**lose from any application's Control menu if you need to quit your program and return to Visual Basic.

Okay people, move along; nothing to see here.

Chapter 8
Adding Pizzazz

In This Chapter

- ☛ Learn about properties
- ☛ Change the font on a control
- ☛ Change the form colors
- ☛ Add VB code to the form

In this chapter, you'll fix up the program you created in Chapter 7, "Your First Application," so that it does more and looks even better. In doing so, you'll learn about changing the properties of controls and the form.

Property Values Are Going Up!

If you saved the program you created in Chapter 7 and quit Visual Basic, start VB and load your program: Select **Open** Project from the File menu, type **FIRST**, and press **Enter** (or choose FIRST.MAK from the file list). Display the form (FORM1.FRM, named by you in Chapter 7) by clicking the View Form command button in the Project window.

A *property* is a characteristic or behavior of a control, form, or other VB element.

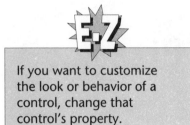

If you want to customize the look or behavior of a control, change that control's property.

The first thing you'll do is change the properties of the command button. Before doing that, take a quick detour to study Figure 8.1. The figure includes three command buttons, not unlike the one in your project. Each of the command buttons, although similar, are also different from each other.

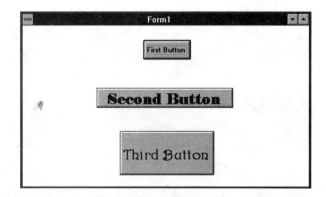

Figure 8.1

Three command buttons with different properties.

Figure 8.1's command buttons differ from one another because their properties differ. One of the command button's properties is its size. Another property is a command button's label. Another property might be the command button's font name or font size. There are many properties for command buttons, some of which are listed in Table 8.1.

Table 8.1   Common Command Button Properties

Property	Description
Caption	The text on the button.
Default	**True** or **False**, depending on whether the command button is the default button (the one with the *focus*) if you don't select another command

Property	Description
	button, using the **Tab** key or mouse. Only one command button on a form can have a Default property set to **True** (as opposed to **False**, which means it's not the default button).
FontBold	**True** or **False**, depending on whether the caption's font is to be boldfaced.
FontItalic	**True** or **False**, depending on whether the caption's font is to be italicized.
FontName	The name of the font used for the caption. If you use True Type fonts within Windows (and you should), those fonts are all available for a command button's font.
FontSize	The size of the font, in *points*. A point is 1/72 of an inch. Standard word processed on-screen text usually ranges from 8 to 12 points.
FontUnderline	**True** or **False**, depending on whether the caption's font is to be underlined.
Height	The height of the command button, usually measured in twips.
Left	The measurement (in those twips again) from the center of the command button to the window's left edge.
Top	The measurement, in twips, from the center of the command button to the window's top edge.
Visible	**True** or **False**, depending on whether the command button is to be visible. (If invisible,

SPEAK LIKE A GEEK

A *twip* is 1/4400 of an inch (very small indeed), and is used for Windows screen measurements.

continues

Table 8.1   Continued

Property	Description
	the Visible property is **False**. Your VB program code can turn the visibility on and off when needed.)
Width	The measurement, in twips, from the command button's left edge to the command button's right edge.

There are a lot more command button properties than those listed in the table. Many of these properties are properties of *other* controls as well. For instance, a Text Label control (a control that simply displays text) has a size, a font, and so forth. A Text Label control does not, however, have a Default property.

> ### Put It to Work
>
> The Properties window holds each control's property settings. Take a look at the Properties window for your program's command buttons, and you'll see the command button's property values.

As you point to a control (for example, if there are several on your form), the Properties window changes to show that control's current values.

You won't always mess with many of the control properties. For example, it is usually easier to use the mouse for moving and resizing command buttons than to type in those property values. In Chapter 7, you didn't have to set any of the properties. By default, when you double-clicked the Command Button control on the toolbox, VB set the Top, Width, and Left properties automatically so the command button appeared in the center of the screen (which is exactly what you wanted at the time).

The default Caption property is always set to **Command1**, **Command2**, and so on, for each command button you add to a form. When you first place a command button, VB assumes that you want to change the Caption property. That's why, when you typed **Hi!** in Chapter 7, as soon as you selected the command button, you saw **Hi!** appear on the command button. You were, unknowingly, replacing the default **Command1** Caption property with **Hi!**.

Figure 8.2 shows the Properties window for your program's command button. You can scroll through the properties, or resize the window (by dragging the top edge), to see more properties at once if you like.

Figure 8.2

The command button's Properties window.

To change a property from within the Properties window, highlight the line that includes the property you want to change. For example, scroll down and highlight the FontSize property. Type **13.5**. (The default value is 8.25.) As you type the numbers, look toward the top of the Properties window, and you'll see **13.5** appearing after the checkmark. That's where changes you make appear until you press **Enter**.

As soon as you change the FontSize property to **13.5** and press **Enter**, **Hi!** immediately grows on your form. You've changed the command button's FontSize property so that the caption is now larger.

You can click the data-entry box's **down arrow** to see a list of FontSize choices, and select the **13.5** font size.

Even the Form Has Properties

Yes, even the form has a Properties window. Click the mouse anywhere on the white form (but not over your command button). Press **F4** (the access key for the Properties option of the **W**indow menu) to bring the form's Properties window into view. You can scroll through the list of form properties.

How about changing the color of the form from the dull white to bright red? (Well, one good reason not to is that most Windows programs use a white background, and you should always maintain consistency to keep conformity with other programs. Also, bright red is really ugly for a form! Nevertheless, this isn't Art Appreciation 101, so give it a try.) Follow these simple steps:

1. Scroll the Properties window so that the BackColor property appears.

2. VB wants to know the numeric color code that you want to enter. White's color code is **&H00FFFFFF&**. If you think that's a weird number, you're right. It's called an *octal* number, and now you can forget all about *that*. Instead of learning every octal number for every possible background color, click the mouse on the ellipsis (...) on the second line of the Properties window. A color chart appears, like the one shown in Figure 8.3.

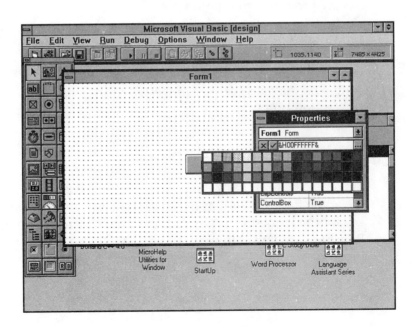

Figure 8.3

Selecting a new form color.

3. Click the bright red color square in the third column of the color table. As soon as you do, the form color changes to bright red, and VB fills in the octal number for you in the BackColor property. When you run the program at the end of this chapter, the form will still be bright red instead of white (as it was when you first ran the program).

Stop Elegantly

Be warned that you may not fully understand this final modification. You're going to add Visual Basic code, an actual programming language statement, to the program.

As your program now stands, there is no elegant way for the user to exit once he or she starts the program. The window control menu button's Close option is not the best way to exit the program. Let's make the command button, labeled **Hi!**, trigger the program's end as soon as the user presses the command button. Follow these steps:

1. Double-click the command button. When you do, a strange window, like the one in Figure 8.4, opens. This window is called the code window.

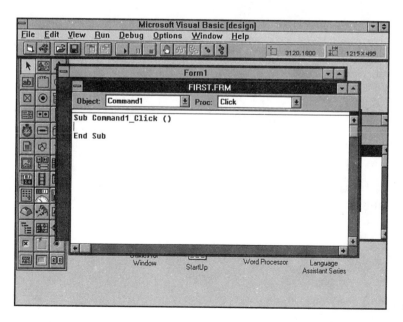

Figure 8.4

The code window opens when you double-click the command button.

The code window holds the code behind the form. You might write 20-page programs for each control or form. The entire VB programming language is large, and you'll hear about it later in this book. For now, perform this example to see how code can control the program.

2. Press **Tab** to indent a few spaces. Type **End**. You've just completed a three-line program (technically, a *subroutine*, which is kind of a miniprogram).

    Look at the top of the code window. You are writing code for the **Command1** object. An object might be a form, control, or another VB element you'll learn about. See the name of the subroutine on the program's first line? **Command1_Click** is the name. This code runs when the user clicks the **Command1** button. These subroutine names always contains two parts, separated by an underscore. The first part of the name is the object's name, and the second part is the action you're writing code for. The default action is **Click**, but there are many ways to write code for other actions, as you'll see later.

3. Now that you've studied the code window, close it by double-clicking on the control button in the upper-left corner (or pressing **Alt+F4**, the access key).

4. Run the program to view your red form.

5. Once you're done admiring your work, point to the **Hi!** command button, and click the mouse. (You could instead press **Enter**, because the command button has the default focus and would click if you pressed **Enter**.) Visual Basic returns to the Form window, where you can save the work or make more changes.

6. Exit the program, and answer **Yes** when VB reminds you that you need to save the form.

7. Take a break, and have ice cream! You now know more about Visual Basic than you probably thought possible before you opened this book.

TECHNO NERD TEACHES...

The **End** command stops a running program whenever VB encounters **End**.

Unlike many programming languages, VB is *event driven*. An event might be virtually anything your user does, such as clicking a mouse button, pressing a key, or moving the mouse. The code you put in your Visual Basic application will always respond to those events.

When you have to write code to perform an action, as you just did with **End** to end the program, you'll add that code in an event *subroutine*. Subroutine is just a fancy term for a small piece of code that runs once in a while.

The Least You Need to Know

The design of your form is only half of a program's creation. You must also specify the appropriate properties of the controls on your form. Even the form itself has properties. Virtually everything you do in Visual Basic modifies property values. You can even write VB code to change properties of virtually any Visual Basic control. For example, you can change the form's color from within the Visual Basic program code you write. This chapter demonstrates one of the easiest VB commands, **End**, and also cleans up the behavior of your program. By adding **End** to the command button's click code, you let the user exit the program by clicking the command button. Here are some things to remember:

- ☞ All controls, forms, and other objects have properties.

- ☞ You change properties from the Properties window.

- ☞ You don't need to enter color values; instead, you can choose from the color selections that Visual Basic displays.

- ☞ **End** is the Visual Basic command to end a program.

Buy Complete Idiot's Guides—They're not just for idiots anymore.

Chapter 9
Labels Describe

In This Chapter

- ☛ Learn to use a new control: the Label control
- ☛ Add a title to your program
- ☛ Add a helpful message that describes the command button
- ☛ Change the properties of labels you place in the application

Surely you want your Windows applications to do more than display a command button and quit. (Some people are just *never* satisfied!) Visual Basic's other toolbox controls are wonderful—they spice up your applications. This chapter builds on your application by putting some labels on the form.

A Label Maker

The Label control displays text on your form. As with a command button, you can control the font style, the font size, the color, and all sorts of other Label control properties. Also, as with all other controls, your application can have lots of Label controls, and you may set different properties for each one.

Command buttons, labels, and text boxes all display text, but each is a different control. You click command buttons to trigger actions, whereas labels do nothing but sit on the form, adding descriptive text (such as instructions and titles), and text boxes display text and give the user a chance to change that text.

If you haven't got your FIRST.MAK application loaded at this time, go ahead and load it now (using the **Open** option of the **File** menu, and you know the rest).

Adding Some Labels

Figure 9.1 shows what the form will look like after you make the changes described next. The figure gives you an idea where this section is heading. In a moment, when you place your own labels, if you don't get them placed *exactly* like the ones in the figure, don't worry, you're among friends. (Yours might look better anyway!)

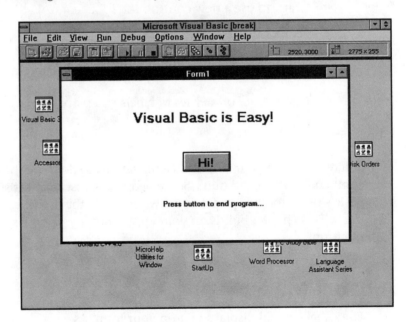

Figure 9.1

A form with Label controls added.

The first thing you'll do is add the title to the top of your application's screen. Any time you want to add text to a window, add the text using a Label control. Remember how you added the Command Button control? You double-clicked the Command Button control on the toolbox, and Visual Basic placed the command button in the center of the screen.

Although you could place the Label control in the same way, if you double-clicked the toolbox's Label control, VB would put the control right on top of the command button that's already in the center of the screen. It's faster at this point to use the alternate method for selecting controls from the toolbox. Follow these steps:

Before going any further, change your form's ugly bright red background back to white, like forms in all good Windows programs. Select the Properties window's BackColor property, click the ... button, and choose white.

1. Click once (don't double-click) the Label control on the toolbox. (That's the control with the capital letter *A*. I'm not going to tell you again.)

2. Move the mouse to the approximate location of the title you see at the top of the window in Figure 9.1. As soon as the mouse cursor hits the form, the cursor changes to a crosshair. Position the crosshair so that it appears at about the same location as the upper-left corner of the title in Figure 9.1.

3. After you position the crosshair, hold down the mouse button and drag the mouse cursor down and to the right. As you drag the mouse, you'll be expanding and lengthening the label that you're placing. When you let up on the mouse button, your screen will look something like the one in Figure 9.2.

If you need to adjust the size of your Label control, drag any of the eight resizing handles until the width and height approximately match those in the figure. If you don't see the resizing handles, click once anywhere inside the label. If you need to move the label, click and hold down the mouse button while pointing anywhere within the label, and drag the label left, right, up, or down.

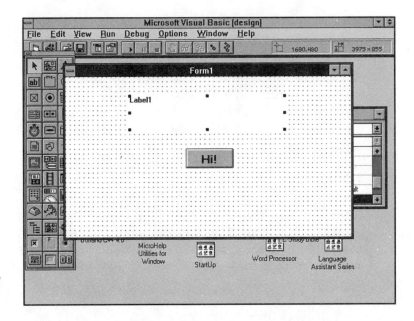

Figure 9.2

A newly placed Label control.

4. Before finalizing that label, go ahead and add the label you saw at the bottom of Figure 9.1. Add this second Label control the same way that you just added the title. You can see that the bottom label is much thinner than the top one, and Visual Basic will place the **Label2** Caption property as the label's title. When you are finished, your form should look like the one in Figure 9.3.

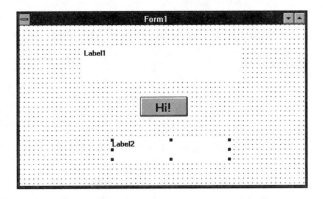

Figure 9.3

A second Label control.

You can click on the top label (which not only displays the label's resizing handles, but also changes the Properties window so it shows that particular Label control's properties), and enter these exact values if you wish your final window to look, *to a twip*, like the window in Figure 9.1.

Put It to Work

If you *really* want to match Figure 9.1's labels in size and placement, here are the Properties window values for the top title label:

Height: 495
Left: 1800
Top: 720
Width: 3735

Here are the Properties window values for the bottom message label:

Height: 255
Left: 2520
Top: 3000
Width: 2775

Honing the Labels

What's next? Now you've got to modify the default labels that VB placed on the form with labels that contain the text shown back in Figure 9.1.

I bet that you already know enough to finalize these labels yourself! Just in case you're not quite sure, follow the instructions.

Obviously, the FontSize property of the top label is larger than that of the bottom label. Furthermore, the Caption properties are not **Label1** and **Label2**. Therefore, perform the following steps to change your two Label controls to those of the final program shown in Figure 9.1:

1. Click the top label. Press **F4** to bring that label's Properties window into focus.

2. Highlight (by pointing with the mouse) the Caption property. Type **Visual Basic is Easy!**. As you type, Visual Basic displays the text in two places: in the actual label on the form and in the second line of the Properties window.

3. The FontSize caption is not set properly. Change the FontSize property to **18**.

4. Another Label control property, the Alignment property, helps keep your text centered in a Label control. Scroll the Properties window upward until the Alignment property comes into view. Click the **down arrow** on the second line of the Properties window (the data-entry area, where your Properties window changes appear). You'll see a list of Alignment property choices like those shown in Figure 9.4.

Figure 9.4

A list of Alignment property choices.

Justification describes text. When left-justified, text appears against the left side of a control. When right-justified, the text appears against the right side of a control. When centered, the text sits right in the middle of a control.

5. Select the Alignment property **2—Center**. The Center Alignment property ensures that the text in the label remains centered no matter how wide or thin you resize the label. You've now finished the top label.

6. The bottom label requires the same treatment. Click the bottom label, and press **F4** to display the Properties window. Change the Caption to **Press button to end program...**, and change the FontSize to **8.25** if it's not already set by default. Finally, change the Alignment property to **2—Center**.

7. Press **F5** to run the program and see the results. Clicking the command button ends the program when you're done. The seventh (from the left) tool on the toolbar shows a **right arrow** that looks a lot like a tape deck's play button. If you click this tool (the Start tool), you run the program just as if you pressed **F5** or selected **Start** from the **Run** menu.

The Least You Need to Know

Anytime you want text to appear on a form (a program's window), use a Label control. Think of the Label control as a holder for each piece of text, as well as all properties about that text. There are all sorts of properties applicable to Label controls that control the font, justification, and style of the text on the label. Here are some things to remember:

☞ You can use the Label control for program text that you want the user to read.

☞ After you resize your Label controls, remember to adjust the text's font size, style, and other properties to make the label look exactly the way you want.

☞ You can use the Alignment Property control for justification, which describes how text fills a control's area.

Unexpected End of File.

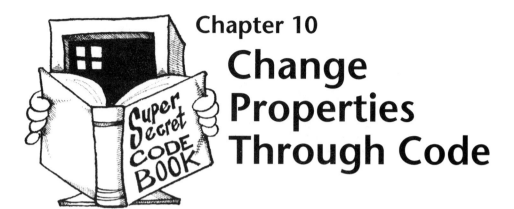

Chapter 10

Change Properties Through Code

In This Chapter

- Learn the assignment statement
- Change properties through code
- Add a second command button to your program
- Control your form's color
- Use the **QBColor()** function and its arguments
- Add borders to labels

This chapter dives a little more into the Visual Basic language. Learning a programming language such as Visual Basic is easier than learning a foreign language—although some absolute beginners wonder if that's the case! Nevertheless, this book will not teach you all there is to know about the Visual Basic programming language, because you don't have to master the entire language to be productive with Visual Basic.

TECHNO NERD TEACHES...

If you've ever studied another programming language, such as QBasic, C, or Pascal, you know that you had to study each programming statement and learn several statements before you could write a simple program. You've already written full-fledged Windows programs, and the only VB statement briefly mentioned so far is **End**!

The Assignment Statement and =

Think of the equals sign as being a left-pointing arrow. Whatever is on the right of the equals sign is sent to the left-hand property.

Almost every programming language contains an assignment statement. An *assignment statement* assigns values to properties. You'll recognize the assignment statement when you see an equals sign (=). Here is the format of an assignment statement:

objectName.property = newValue

Whenever you see a VB statement's format, such as the assignment statement's format, you'll have to replace the italicized text with something else. For example, you must supply something in place of *objectName*. A VB object might be a form or a control. Each object has a name. The form you've been working on has the name Form1, although you can change an object's name through the object's Properties window.

Put It to Work

If you click on your form and press **F4** to see the Properties window, you'll see that the Name property contains **Form1**. If you click on the command button and press **F4**, you'll see that the command button's name is **Command1**. You can change the name by entering a new value for the Name property.

Replace *property* with the named object's property that you want to change. For example, if you wanted to change the Caption property of the form, you might put this on the left of the equals sign: **Form1.Caption**. If you had changed the form's Name property to MyForm, you'd put this on the left of the equals sign: **MyForm.Caption**.

The *newValue* must be any possible value that the object's property can contain. For example, a command button's FontBold property can take on only one of two values: **True** or **False** (a font is either bold or it's not). Therefore, the following assignment statement boldfaces the command button's text: **Command1.FontBold = True**.

If the text were bold and you wanted, through an assignment statement, to remove the boldface from the text, you would enter this: **Command1.FontBold = False**.

TECHNO NERD TEACHES...

You now know two ways to change an object's property. You can enter a new property value directly in the Properties window. You can also use an assignment statement to change the property. Which one should you use?

The answer is that you'll use both. When you design and create an application, you'll set many of the properties at that time. Sometimes, during the *running* of that application, you'll need properties to change in response to the user's actions. When your user runs a program you create, you can't interrupt the user and change properties! Therefore, the VB code that you add to your application (at the time that you design the application), will take care of changing what needs to be changed at runtime.

Prepare Your Program for Assignment

Now you can add a new command button to your FIRST.MAK application. The command button will do nothing more than change the background color of the form. As you know, the form's background starts as white, and

Notice that VB automatically names the second command button **Command2**, and assigns the button's Caption property the same name.

the extra command button, when pressed, will change the color to green. Actually, the button won't change the color, but the code behind the button's Double-Click event will change the color. Before adding the code, you've got to add the button, so please follow these steps:

1. Click the Command Button control on the toolbox.

2. Move the crosshair mouse cursor to the center bottom of the form, beneath the label that reads **Press button to end program....**

3. Size the command button so it looks like the one shown in Figure 10.1.

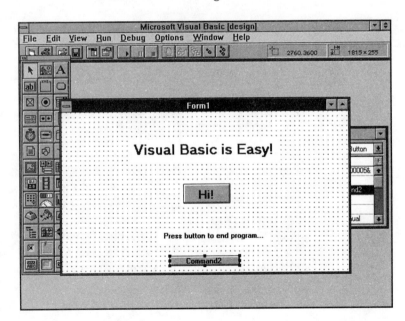

Figure 10.1

A form with a second command button added.

4. Press **F4** to see the second command button's Properties window.

5. Change the Caption property to **Color change**. The command button on the form reads **Color change** to show the new caption.

Adding the Code

That second command button will just sit on the form, doing nothing, until you add another event-driven subroutine. You added another event-driven subroutine to the first command button in Chapter 8, "Adding Pizzazz." The subroutine was small and contained only the **End** statement. The program ended when the user pressed that button. By adding an event-driven subroutine to the second command button, you can have the form's color change when the user presses the button. Perform the following steps to add code to the command button:

VB displays the second command button's code because the second command button had the focus (you were working with that button when you displayed the code). If you had been working on the form or the other command button, the code window for the form or command button would have displayed instead.

1. Select Code from the View menu (**F7** is the access key). You'll see the second command button's code screen, as shown in Figure 10.2.

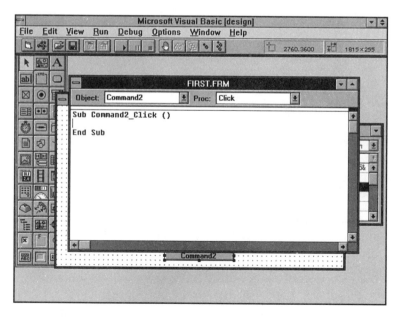

Figure 10.2

Getting ready to add code to a form.

A *text editor* is like a simple word processor.

The code window contains a text editor. Using the **arrow** keys, the **Insert** key, and the **Delete** key, you can enter lines of code just as you would with a word processor.

2. Notice what VB named this subroutine: **Command2_Click()**. (Ignore the parentheses for now, they're really advanced and not worth worrying about at this time.) You can tell from the name that this code executes if the user clicks the second command button. Just for grins, click the **down arrow** to the right of the code window's **Proc:** data-entry box. You'll see all kinds of events that you can select and write code for, such as KeyPress, DragDrop, and MouseDown. VB selected the Click event because clicking is the most common event users do with command buttons. (There's yet another way to open the command button's code window. You could double-click the second command button, and VB would open the code window.)

3. Press **Tab**, and type the following line between the **Sub** and the **End Sub** statements:

   Form1.BackColor = QBColor(2)

   Your Command2.Click subroutine now looks like this:

   Sub Command2_Click ()
     Form1.BackColor = QBColor(2)
   End Sub

   The tab helps separate the subroutine's first and last lines from the body of the subroutine, where the work is done. Later, you'll write subroutines that contain several statements, and the indentation helps make the code more readable.

4. Close the subroutine code window by double-clicking its upper-left window button. Press **F5** to start the program. You see the usual program, but now there is the second button.

5. Click the second command button, and, *Ecco!* (That's Italian for *Wow, look at that!*), the form changes to a nice green color. After you're done admiring your work, click the middle command button to end the program's execution.

The first line of every subroutine is **Sub *SubName***, and the last line is always **End Sub**. You now know a total of four VB programming statements: **End**, the assignment with **=**, **Sub *SubName***, and **End Sub**.

What's That QBColor(2) Thing Doing in My Program?

We kind of hurried right by the right side of the previous program's assignment. Here is the complete statement you just added:

Form1.BackColor = QBColor(2)

Anytime you see parentheses after a Visual Basic name, such as **QBColor()**, whether those parentheses have something in them or not, you're looking at a VB subroutine or function. **QBColor()** happens to be a function, but the difference between a function and subroutine isn't important at this time.

You've filled in two of your own subroutines, **Command1_Click()** and **Command2_Click()**. There are lots of subroutines and functions that you don't have to write—the developers of VB wrote them for you. **QBColor()** is such a function.

> **What have you got now? A program with two command buttons. Code behind the second command button enables the user to change the form's color. Code behind the first command button enables the user to end the program. The user doesn't have to change the color; the first command button is not related to the second. If you start the program, run it, and press only the first button, the program terminates without the form's color ever changing.**

You use **QBColor()** when you want to assign a color value to a property. If you look at any Properties window, you'll see as a BackColor a weird-looking octal number that corresponds to a color value. It would be nice if you could just type the words **Red** or **Blue** when you want to specify a color, but there are just too many shades possible for such simple descriptions. Nevertheless, VB has reserved the 16 colors shown in Table 10.1 to give you a semieasy way to specify common colors. The value in Table 10.1 corresponds to the color you want to specify. When you insert the value inside **QBColor()**'s parentheses, you are, in effect, specifying a color from the table. Using **QBColor()** means you can stay away from weird octal numbers!

A *function* is a lot like a subroutine in that it's a small section of code that executes when a certain event happens. For now, you can consider a function and subroutine to be the same thing.

The reason your program's form changes to green when you press the second command button is that you typed **2** inside **QBColor()**'s parentheses.

Table 10.1 QBColor() Values and Their Meanings

Value	Color
0	Black
1	Blue
2	Green
3	Cyan
4	Red
5	Magenta
6	Yellow
7	White
8	Gray
9	Light blue
10	Light green
11	Light cyan
12	Light red
13	Light magenta
14	Light yellow
15	Bright white

If a value appears inside a subroutine or function's parentheses, the value is called an *argument*. The **QBColor()** argument in your program is **2**.

One Last Tip

Here's a suggestion that you'll find handy at times. So far, your form's labels have had no borders, making them blend right in with the form's background. You can easily add a border to any label to make the label stand out, by changing the label's BorderStyle property to **1—Fixed Single**, instead of the default **0—None**. Figure 10.3 shows the FIRST application running with the bottom label, the one instructing the user to end the program, bordered.

The **0** or **1** before the border style is all you need to assign when changing the label's BorderStyle with code. In other words, you can either assign **1** or **1—Fixed Single** when using an assignment statement to add a border to a label.

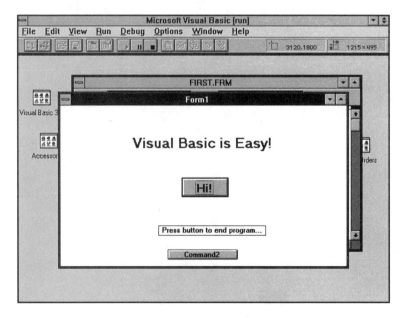

Figure 10.3

Labels with borders added.

The Least You Need to Know

Hey, you're really coming along! You're adding code left and right, and you're really doing a lot with that VB program. How much knowledge would you say you have now? a lot? If you still don't think you're working hard enough, that's the idea. There's a lot to Visual Basic, but you don't have to know everything to get results. Here are some of the things you've learned:

☛ The assignment statement's format is

objectName.property = newValue

☛ The assignment statement enables your code to change property values.

☛ Each subroutine that you write is independent of the others. What takes place in one has little bearing on what the others do, until you write really advanced programs and start linking some of the functions together.

☛ **QBColor()** is a built-in VB function that enables you to easily specify 1 of 16 color values.

☛ You can add borders to your labels with the BorderStyle property.

Chapter 11

Text Boxes Get Input

In This Chapter

- ☛ Use Text Box controls to get the user's text
- ☛ Build a comprehensive program that contains a form with four Command Button controls, five Label controls, and two Text Box controls
- ☛ Add code to change text entered by the user
- ☛ Display the user's text in the changed format

So far, your program has produced a lot of output; you've seen screen messages and command buttons produced by the program. You've even (while acting as the *user* and not as the *programmer*) given your program some input by clicking command buttons. In response to that input, your program has acted accordingly, either by changing the form's colors or by ending the program.

Input is any data, keystrokes, or mouse movements sent to your program, as opposed to *output*, which is data you see on the screen, data sent to the printer, or data sent to a disk file from your program.

There is more to input than mouse clicks. This chapter shows you how to get text data from your user. You'll learn how the user can type data on the keyboard and let your program grab that data and work with it. The Text Box tool provides the input area where the user's entered text appears.

Visual Basic names Text Box controls **Text1**, **Text2**, and so on. As with Command Button and Label controls, you can rename Text Box controls and change their captions.

If you can't match the exact placement of these controls on your own form, that's okay—this isn't brain surgery! Just get the controls on the form so they look somewhat like those in the figure so you can complete the rest of this chapter.

Adding Text Boxes

Adding a Text Box control is easy, because you add Text Box controls in the same way that you add Label controls. Just double-clicking the Text Box control (the control with the lowercase letters *ab*) puts a text box in the center of the form. If you already have something in the center of the form, you're better off clicking the Text Box control once to highlight the control, then moving the crosshair mouse cursor to place and size the control the way you want it.

Figure 11.1 shows a new form that you need to create for this chapter's program. The Text Box and Label controls all have borders (their BorderStyle property is set to **1**), so you can see where the controls go and how to resize them. When you finish adding these controls, save the form and program's project file under the names MYNAME.FRM and MYNAME.MAK.

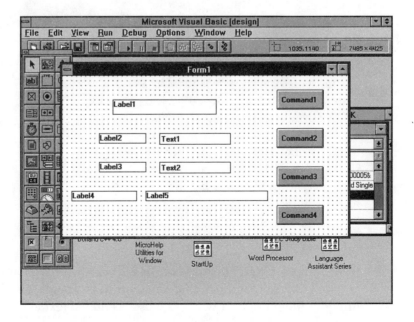

Figure 11.1

Beginning a new program.

Cleaning Up the Form

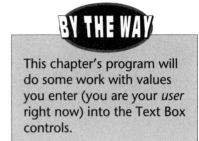

Now that you've designed the layout of your form, take a few moments to add some needed labels and property settings to the controls you added in the previous section. Your goal is to get your form to look like the one in Figure 11.2. Sure, some of the labels might seem cryptic at this point, but the remainder of the chapter explains what this application is going to do.

This chapter's program will do some work with values you enter (you are your *user* right now) into the Text Box controls.

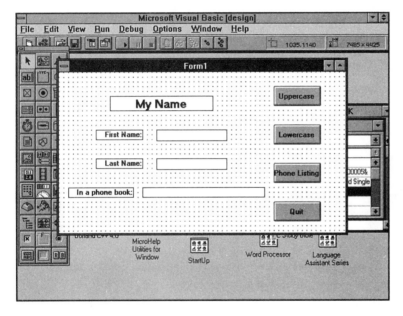

Figure 11.2

The details you'll add to the form.

Perhaps you'd like to try adding the form details of Figure 11.2 to your form yourself. Try it. If you mess up, you can always reload the form you created in the last section (you named it MYNAME). If you can fix up the form yourself, great, go to the next section. However, don't be embarrassed if you have to rely on the following steps:

1. Click the top label (**Label1**) to highlight the label. Press **F4** to display the label's Properties window.

2. Change the Alignment property to **2—Center**. Change the Caption to **My Name**. Change the FontSize to 13.5.

3. In a like manner, highlight and display the Properties window for the second label (**Label2**). Change the Alignment property to **1—Right**. This ensures that your caption is right-justified (scooted up against the right border). Change the Caption property to **First Name:**.

4. Change **Label3**'s Alignment property to **1—Right**. Change the Caption property to **Last Name:**.

5. Change **Label4**'s Alignment property to **1—Right**. Change the Caption property to **In a phone book:**.

6. Highlight the first Text Box control, which is named **Text1**. Press **F4** to display its Properties window. Instead of typing a new caption, highlight the Text property as if you were going to type a new caption, and then press the **Del** key (or press **Backspace** several times) to completely erase the caption.

Changing the Caption property does not change the Name property. The Caption and Name properties start off with the same name, but the Caption property only determines what text appears on the control, not the control's name.

7. Erase the caption for the second Text Box control as well.

8. Erase the caption for the fifth label (**Label5**).

9. Change the Caption property on each of the four command buttons, from top to bottom (**Command1** to **Command4**), to **Uppercase, Lowercase, Phone Listing,** and **Quit**.

10. Save the form again, under the name MYNAME.

Give Command Buttons Power

Now that you've mastered form creation (you have mastered it, right?), you're ready to delve more deeply into the underlying VB code. You're now going to add some code to each of the four command buttons. The last command button is easy because its code will match that of your last application's (FIRST.MAK) command button.

Highlight the fourth command button. You need to add code to the button's Click event (the most common event that happens to command buttons). Remember, there are three ways to display the code text-editing window behind the button:

- ☞ Select Code from the View menu.
- ☞ Press **F7** (the speedkey for selecting Code from the View menu).
- ☞ Double-click the command button on the form.

In all three cases, VB displays the **Command4_Click()** subroutine, because that's the most common event that will take place. (Later, you'll write code for other events listed in the **Proc:** pull-down menu on the code screen.) Add the **End** statement to the subroutine so it reads like this:

```
Sub Command4_Click ()
    End
End Sub
```

Return to the form by clicking anywhere on the underlying form's window (if you can see the Form window under the code window) or by double-clicking the code window's control button in the upper-left corner of the window.

Did you remember to press **Tab** before typing **End**?

Now, you need to add code to the other three command buttons. Display the first command button's code window so it looks like the following:

```
Sub Command1_Click ()
    Text1.Text = UCase(Text1.Text)
    Text2.Text = UCase(Text2.Text)
End Sub
```

Display the second command button's code window so it looks like the following:

```
Sub Command2_Click ()
    Text1.Text = LCase(Text1.Text)
    Text2.Text = LCase(Text2.Text)
End Sub
```

You probably won't understand the code yet. The next section explains the code.

Display the third command button's code window so it looks like the following:

```
Sub Command3_Click ()
    Label5.Caption = Text2.Text + ", " + Text1.Text
End Sub
```

You've done it! You've now created a truly interactive program. Although the code might be a little cryptic yet, you'll be surprised at how much it does. Save your program one more time, under the name MYNAME.

Notice that the Label controls identify what the Text Box controls are to hold. Never get data from your user without putting next to the text box a descriptive label that tells the user what kind of data you want entered.

Run the program to display your form. As soon as Visual Basic runs the program, notice where the cursor appears. You'll find the cursor at the start of the first text box. Visual Basic is waiting for you, the user, to type data. Before, you couldn't enter text onto your forms (except at design time), because there were only labels and command buttons.

Type your first name. When you are finished typing your name, press **Tab**. VB sends the cursor down to the next Text Box control. Type your last name.

Press **Tab** again. Where's the cursor? You'll see that the top command button (**Uppercase**) is now highlighted. Why didn't the cursor fall down to the blank label at the bottom of the screen? Of course! VB knows that you can't enter text into a label, so VB never puts the cursor there.

Click the **Uppercase** command button, and look at your first and last name. Wow! They are now uppercased! Now click the **Lowercase** command button, and they're both lowercased.

The third command button shows how your name appears in a phone book (last name first). Click the **Phone Listing** button, and see the text label at the bottom of the screen contain your phone listing.

After putting your name in lowercase, the listing doesn't look right, but that's fine for now. You should be getting the idea that there is code working behind your form to produce the results that you see.

To quit and return to the form, click the **Quit** button, and take a break.

Just a Little Explanation

In the previous chapter, you learned about a built-in VB function named **QBColor()**. When you put a color number argument in the parentheses, VB responds by running the function and changing the **QBColor()** to an octal value so you don't have to.

Of course, you didn't have to click either the **Upper-case** or **Lowercase** button before clicking the third one. If you had typed your first and last names as you normally do, by capitalizing the first letter, then went immediately to the third command button, you'd see your name uppercased correctly in the bottom label.

The two functions used in the first two command buttons are UCase() and **LCase()**. As their names suggest, they take whatever argument you list in their parentheses and convert that argument to either uppercase or lowercase letters.

TECHNO NERD TEACHES...

A function *becomes* its *return value*. That's techie talk meaning the following: When you pass an argument to a function, you are telling the function to take that argument and convert that argument to something else. The job of **UCase()**, for example, is to convert its argument to uppercase, and then become that converted uppercased text.

Consider the following assignment found in **Command1**'s **Command1_Click()** subroutine:

```
Text1.Text = UCase(Text1.Text)
```

If you had changed the Text Box control names to **FirstText** and **LastText**, there would have been more to type, but the names would have made more sense and been easier to remember. In that case, the previous line of code would read like this:

FirstText.Text = UCase(FirstText.Text)

Do you remember the control named **Text1**? It's the control that holds your first name. The Text property holds the text typed by the user (or nothing if the user has yet to type anything, because you blanked out the Text property when you designed the form). You are assigning a *new value* to the Text property of the **Text1** control. The new value is simply the old value of the text box sent to **UCase()**. **UCase()** converts that value to uppercase letters. The converted uppercase text is assigned to the text box, where you see the uppercase on the screen.

Scan the second command button's code window, and study the way **LCase()** is used there.

The *harder* (not really) code appears in the **Phone Listing** command button. Actually, the line is just a simple assignment statement. Here is the one-line body of the code:

Label5.Caption = Text2.Text + ", " + Text1.Text

Look at what's being assigned to the bottom label's (**Label5**) Caption property: the *second* text box's text (the last name), followed by a comma and space inside quotation marks, followed by the text in the first text box (which holds the first name). The plus sign (+) strings these three values together.

Concatenation is a silver dollar word that means stringing one chunk of text together with another chunk of text to form a single, longer chunk of text.

VB uses the plus sign for math, and it also uses the plus sign to concatenate text. If numbers appear on each side of the plus sign, VB performs addition. If text appears, VB performs string concatenation. (You'll learn more about the plus sign in Chapter 14, "Variables Don't Stay the Same.")

The Least You Need to Know

You're really productive now! You've created a form that manipulates text behind the scenes whenever the user clicks on a command button. You've also explored two more functions, **UCase()** and **LCase()**, which convert text to uppercase and lowercase, respectively. Here are some things you've learned:

- ☞ Use the Text Box control when you want user input.

- ☞ The **UCase()** and **LCase()** functions change their arguments to uppercase and lowercase letters.

- ☞ The plus sign performs concatenation when embedded between two text values.

Meditation page (insert mantra here)

Chapter 12

Advanced Labels and Text Boxes

In This Chapter

- ☞ Create expanding and shrinking Label controls
- ☞ Control the word wrap of labels
- ☞ Give your user default text box values
- ☞ Display multiline Text Box controls
- ☞ Add scroll bars to large Text Box controls
- ☞ Display default multiline text box text

This chapter sharpens your label and Text Box controls skills so that you can create forms with any and all information you need. The Label and Text Box controls you've put in your programs have been one-liners, but what if you want to send more than one line of text to a label? You could simply add more Label controls, storing one line of the message in each control, but that would be silly when a single Label control can hold several lines of text.

Always-Changing Label Sizes

When you write your program, if you know exactly what text will appear inside a Label control, you can size that control at that time so it will hold all the text. Look at the label placed in the form in Figure 12.1. Obviously, the label should have more space dedicated because not all the text will fit in the label.

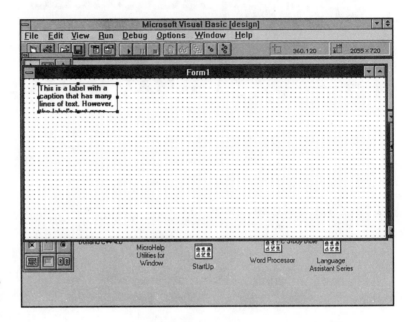

Figure 12.1

Too much text for the Label control's size.

If you set the WordWrap property to **True**, but don't set the AutoSize property to **True**, neither vertical nor horizontal resizing will occur. Nevertheless, the last word inside the Label control will not be cut off midword, as might happen with WordWrap set to **False**. VB removes any partial word that might appear at the end of the Label control, instead of displaying only one or a few characters of the word.

Here is the text that was typed for Figure 12.1's label Caption property:

This is a label with a caption that has many lines of text. However, the label's text goes past the size.

There are two ways to expand the size of the Label control shown in Figure 12.1 (besides using the mouse at program creation time). The AutoSize and WordWrap properties determine how the label will change. Keep in mind the following:

☞ If you want a Label control to stay the same size as you designed it, make sure the AutoSize property is set to **False** (the default) when you add the label to the form. No matter how the text changes during the running of the program, the boundaries of the Label control will remain the same size.

☞ If you want the label to expand vertically (down the screen), set both the AutoSize and WordWrap properties to **True**. Figure 12.2 shows what would happen if the Label control AutoSize property in Figure 12.1 were set to **True**.

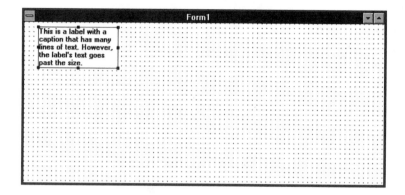

Figure 12.2

Expanding vertically with AutoSize and WordWrap.

☞ If you want the label to expand horizontally (across the screen), set the AutoSize property to **True**, but leave the WordWrap property set to **False**.

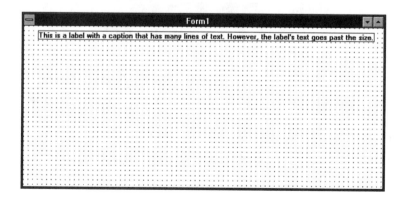

Figure 12.3

Expanding horizontally with AutoSize.

Advanced Text Labels

Although the previous chapter taught you about Text Box controls, the Text Box controls you added to the MYNAME application intially had Text properties that were blank. The user filled in those blanks with the user's first and last names.

Instead of blanking out a Text Box control's Text property, you might want to display an initial text box contents. This would be the default text box contents that the user sees inside the text box when the program runs. If the user doesn't want to change the contents of the text box, the user doesn't have to enter new text.

> ## Put It to Work
> Load the MYNAME application that you created in the previous chapter. Change the Text properties for both the **Text1** and **Text2** Text Box controls to hold **J.** and **Smith**. When the user (you!) then runs the program, the user sees the names shown in Figure 12.4.

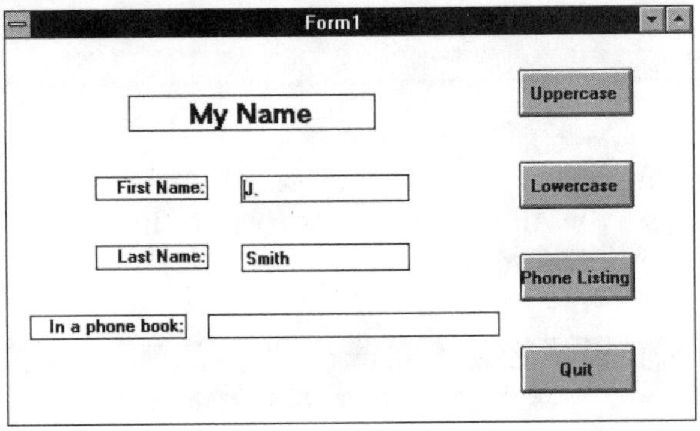

Figure 12.4

Default Text properties in the Text Box controls.

The text cursor will appear at the **J.** in the first name Text Box control, but you don't have to replace that **J.** with anything else when you run the program. If you run the program with these two default Text Box control properties, and press either the **Uppercase** or **Lowercase** command button, the **J.** and **Smith** will convert to uppercase or lowercase.

If you set the MultiLine property of a Text Box control to **True**, the user can enter more than one line of text. The ScrollBars property also has to be set to something other than the default of **0—None**. You are familiar with scroll bars because you see them in virtually every Windows program.

Consider the Text Box control shown in Figure 12.5. The text box has two scroll bars, a horizontal scroll bar and a vertical scroll bar. The scroll bars are easy to add to a multiline Text Box control, because you only have to specify one of the following values in the ScrollBars property when you design the program and set the Text Box control's properties:

Default text box contents are useful for data-entry screens for address entries. If you write a program that accepts customer information, such as name and address, and if most of your customers reside in the same city, you might want to default the city and state Text Box controls to your city and state. If a customer buys something but lives in a different city, the data-entry clerk can always replace the default value with the customer's city.

☞ Set the Text Box control's ScrollBars property to **0—None** if you don't want to allow for any scroll bars.

☞ Set the Text Box control's ScrollBars property to **1—Horizontal** if you want to allow for horizontal scroll bars across the bottom of the Text Box control.

☞ Set the Text Box control's ScrollBars property to **2—Vertical** if you want to allow for vertical scroll bars down the right side of the text box.

☞ Set the Text Box control's ScrollBars property to **3—Both** if you want both a horizontal and a vertical scroll bar.

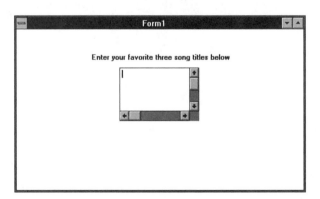

Figure 12.5

A powerful multiline Text Box control.

Given the text box in Figure 12.5, the user doesn't have to press **Enter** at the end of each song title, because the text box scrolls horizontally as the user types. Only after each song is finished does the user have to press **Enter** to move the cursor down (vertically) to the next line of the text box.

The MultiLine property must be set to **True** for the Scroll Bars property to go into effect. After all, no matter how large the text box is, if the MultiLine property is **False**, which is the default, scrollbars aren't very useful.

You Want an Initial Multiline Text Box?

No matter how hard you try, you cannot enter a multiline Text Box control value. In other words, you cannot add a large multiline text box and put a multiline description in the box at design time. As a matter of fact, the MultiLine property is set to **True**, which means that no default Text property will appear at all, not even a short one-line word or phrase.

Here's the dilemma: You want to display default text in a text box, but the MultiLine property keeps any text from showing when you run the program. You *must* specify such default text with VB code. The best place to do this is in a special subroutine that VB calls every time a program is run and a form is loaded (to be displayed). The subroutine is named **Form_Load()**. The bottom line is this: To add initial multiline text to a Text Box control's Text property, you must use an assignment statement in **Form_Load**.

Even the form has events. Windows must load your form (hence the name **Form_Load()**) when you run your program.

To get to the **Form_Load()** subroutine, double-click anywhere on the form's white background as you write your program. You'll see the opening and closing statements for the **Form_Load()** subroutine. Consider the following **Form_Load()** subroutine:

```
Sub Form_Load()
  Text1.text = "I am Alfred. I am a butler. I know  secrets."
End Sub
```

If the **Text1** Text Box control is set with the MultiLine property set to **True**, and the ScrollBars property is set up for horizontal scroll bars (and optionally vertical scroll bars), that long line of text appears in the Text Box control as soon as the program runs (well, as soon as the form loads, which is right at the start of the program's execution).

But wait! Figure 12.6 shows how this message ends up in the text box.

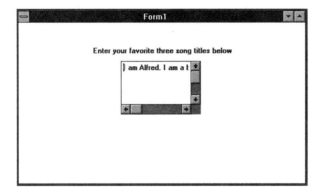

Figure 12.6

The message must be scrolled for you to see it all.

Perhaps you'd like to see the message actually broken into several lines so that the entire message shows in the box. The way you break the message is *really* goofy, but you must do it. Instead of the **Form_Load()** subroutine shown earlier, the following will do a better job at fitting the entire initial message inside the text box:

```
Sub Form_Load ()
  Text1.Text = "I am Alfred." + Chr(13) + Chr(10) +
➥ "I am a butler." + Chr(13) + Chr(10) + "I know secrets."
End Sub
```

Now the message box contents look like those of Figure 12.7. Much better, huh?

The *ASCII table* assigns a numeric, coded value to every possible character your PC can produce. (See Appendix A, "ASCII Table," for an ASCII table.)

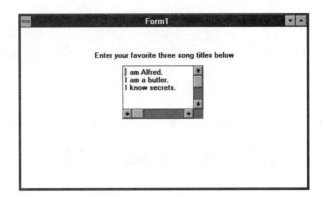

Figure 12.7

The message box now contains all of the message.

Obviously, the line breaks occur at the position of the **Chr(13) + Chr(10)**. Therefore, anytime you want line breaks to appear, in a Text Box control's initial default text insert **Chr(13) + Chr(10)** at the location of those line breaks.

ASCII is pronounced "ask-ee." ASCII does stand for something: *American Standard Code for Information Interchange.* Who cares? Just call it ASCII.

Why not just press **Enter** where the **Enter** goes, instead of messing with that **Chr(13) + Chr(10)** stuff? Good question. In the editor, when writing the **Form1_Load()** subroutine, if you press **Enter**, the *text editor's* cursor (not the resulting message) goes to the text editor's next line. The **Chr()** ensures that the running program's text cursor goes to the next line at the location of each **Chr(13) + Chr(10)**.

Okay, you're about to throw this book away unless you understand what those silly-looking **Chr(13) + Chr(10)** statements mean. Well, the ASCII table shows that the number 13 stands for a *carriage return*, which is nothing more than a request to move the cursor to the far left side of the text box (or label or screen or whatever the cursor resides in at the time). The number 10 stands for a *line feed*, which is a request to move the cursor to the next line. The **Chr()** is a built-in function (just as **UCase()** and **LCase()** are) that converts its argument to the ASCII action or character that matches that argument number.

The Least You Need to Know

Hopefully, you feel like an expert with labels and text boxes. You know just about everything there is to know that's important! So far, you've spent a lot of time learning only these three controls: Label controls, Text Box controls, and Command Button controls. There's a good reason that you've spent so much time on them: Those are the three most common controls in most VB applications. Here are some important topics you now know about:

- The AutoSize and WordWrap properties control label text.

- Give your user common default text box values to lighten the user's burden of data entry.

- Change the text box ScrollBars property if you want the user to be able to enter and view lots of text inside text boxes.

- You must use ASCII table values when inserting line breaks in initial multiline text box text.

**No, this is not a printing error.
The page truly is blank.**

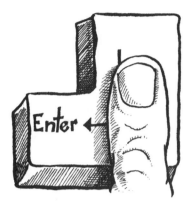

Chapter 13

Command Button Access Keys

In This Chapter

- Access keys ease your user's data-entry burden

- Access keystrokes require an ampersand (&) in the caption

- Access keys for Label controls help to move the focus directly to a Text Box control

Access keys are often called *speedkeys* or *shortcut keys* in other Windows applications. You've already used some access keys when selecting from the Visual Basic menu. For example, to display the File menu, you can click on File or you can press **Alt+F**. The letter that is underlined on the screen is the letter you use with **Alt**, instead of clicking with the mouse, to call up the menu. This chapter shows you how to add access keystroke combinations to your application's command buttons. To practice, you'll change the MYNAME program that you created two chapters ago.

Press Q to Quit

Load your MYNAME program. The program contains four command buttons. You'll add an access key to the most important of these command

I'm calling the command button **Quit** just because **Quit** is the command button's caption. The button is really named **Command4**, unless you changed the Name property when you created the application.

The ampersand does not have to appear before the first letter. Any letter in the caption can be the access key letter.

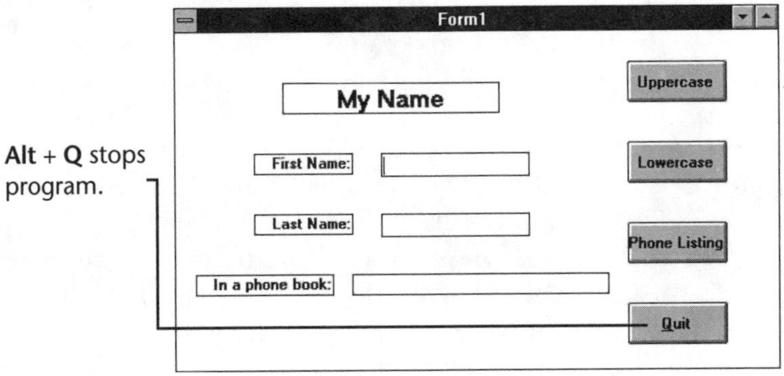

buttons: the **Quit** command button. After adding the access key, the user running the program can select this command in one of the following three ways:

☞ Press **Tab** until the **Quit** command button gets the focus, and then press **Enter**.

☞ Click the **Quit** command button.

☞ Press **Alt+Q**.

To add an access key, all you have to do is put an ampersand (&) before the key's letter in the Caption property. For example, if you change the Caption property of the **Command4** command button to read **&Quit**, you've done all you need to do to add that **Alt+Q** access key. Easy! Figure 13.1 shows the MYNAME application after changing the Caption property for the fourth command button to **&Quit**.

Alt + Q stops program.

Figure 13.1
You can now use Alt+Q to quit the program.

The more access keys you add to your application's command buttons, the happier your users will be (and the more often they'll pay you to write programs for them!). Therefore, get in the habit of adding access keys when you enter your command buttons' Caption properties.

If you want to add access keys to each of the four command button Caption properties in the MYNAME application, you could use these Caption properties:

Don't duplicate access keystrokes. If two command button captions start with the same letter, make a letter other than the first letter the access key for one of the command buttons.

- ☛ **&Uppercase**

- ☛ **&Lowercase**

- ☛ **&Phone Listing**

- ☛ **&Quit**

Put It to Work

For practice, go ahead and add these ampersands to the application and run the program to see the results.

Text Boxes Can Have Access Keys

You can add access keys to Label controls. You cannot enter any text in a Label control, nor can you click a label as you can with Command Button controls. Nevertheless, there is a useful purpose for adding access keys to Label controls: You can force a quick cursor jump (and therefore the focus can be set) to a text box located next to the label with the access key.

In the MYNAME application, there are only two text boxes, and they are the first two places visited by the cursor when you run the program. In computer VB terminology, the *tab index* causes the cursor to appear in these two text boxes before the command buttons receive the focus.

During program development, every time you add a new control to the form, that control receives a TabIndex setting that's one more than the previous control. In other words, your first control's TabIndex property is set to **0**, the next control you add has a TabIndex property of **1**, and so on.

continues

continued

It doesn't matter where you place the controls. If you physically place the third control between the first two, the third control will still automatically have a TabIndex property of **2** (which is the third number, because the first was **0**).

Not every control can receive a focus. You'll remember that *focus* is the term used for a control that is highlighted or has a cursor. In other words, when you run a program and press **Tab**, either the cursor moves to a new text box, or a command button is highlighted. No Label controls are ever highlighted no matter what their TabIndex setting happens to be, because Label controls cannot have the focus.

You can change a Label control's TabIndex property. If you change a TabIndex property, Visual Basic ensures that no other control has that TabIndex. If you use a TabIndex already in use, Visual Basic changes the other control's TabIndex to a different value.

As long as a text box has a descriptive label, as the text boxes in MYNAME have (the labels are **First name:** and **Last name:**), you can add access keystrokes to the labels, and the cursor jumps to the Text Box control next to that label. But...this works only if the label's TabIndex property is one less than the text box's TabIndex property value.

Modifying MYNAME will clear all this up. Here are the goals of this modification:

- ☞ Add an access key, **Alt+F**, to the **First Name:** label so that when the user presses **Alt+F**, no matter where the focus is at the time, the cursor jumps back to the text box at the right of the **First Name:** label.

- ☞ Add an access key, **Alt+A**, to the **Last Name:** label so that when the user presses **Alt+A**, the second text box receives the focus.

When back at the program's design mode (as opposed to running the program), click on the **First Name:** Label control, press **F4**, and look at the

TabIndex property. It is set to **1** because that label was the second control you added to the form. While displaying the properties, change the caption to read **&First Name:**. You'll see that Visual Basic underscores the *F* in the label to show that it's now an access key.

Click on the Text Box control to the immediate right of the **First Name:** label. You'll see that its TabIndex property is set to **4**. Change the TabIndex property to **2**, just one more than the label to the left (that you just added an access keystroke to in the previous paragraph).

The **Last Name:** Label control's TabIndex property now goes to **3**, as you'll see if you click the label and press **F4** to see its Properties window. Change the caption to **L&ast Name:**, and you'll see that Visual Basic underscores the *a* to show that **Alt+A** is the new access key. You want the focus to jump to the text box at the right when the user presses **Alt+A**. Therefore, display the text box's Properties window, and change its TabIndex property to **4** (one more than the label on the left).

Why wouldn't **Alt+L** be a good candidate for the **Last Name:** label? **Alt+L** is already in use; **Alt+L** is the access key for the **Lowercase** command button if you made the change suggested earlier.

Without an access key, you'd have to point to the first name Text Box control with the mouse, or keep pressing **Shift+Tab** until that Text Box control got the focus again.

Don't worry how these TabIndex changes affect the rest of the form. The only two controls whose TabIndexes are modified by these changes are the two at the bottom of the screen. These two controls never receive the focus, so their TabIndex value is meaningless to this application.

If you don't ensure that the text box has a TabIndex value one more than the corresponding Label control that has the access keystroke, the access key could very easily cause the focus to jump to a control unrelated to the label.

When you run the program, you'll see a window like the one in Figure 13.2, with access keys for each action the user can perform.

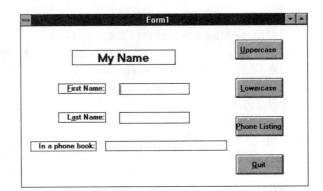

Figure 13.2

After adding access keys to every Text Box and Command Button control.

Why doesn't the bottom label need an access key? Everything else has an access key. Well, that's been answered already in this chapter! The bottom two controls are both labels, not Text Box or Command Button controls. Therefore, an access key would be meaningless because neither of these two controls ever receives the focus.

Put It to Work

Run the program. Follow these steps to see what you just did:

1. Type your first name.

2. Press **Tab** to move to the last name text box. Type your last name.

3. Press **Tab** to move the focus to the top command button. Click this button (with the mouse, or you can just press **Enter**, because the command button has the focus). Your name becomes uppercased.

4. Press **Alt+F**. The cursor immediately jumps back to your first name! You can change the name or type a new one.

5. Press **Alt+L** to convert the names to lowercase.

6. Get the focus back to the last name Text Box control by pressing **Alt+A**. You should be getting the idea.

The Least You Need to Know

Your users will appreciate the addition of access keys in the applications you write for them. Sure, most users will have a mouse, and most can press **Tab** and **Shift**+**Tab** to move the focus from control to control. Nevertheless, there are times when the mouse is faster and there are times when an access keystroke is faster. Give your users the choice, and they'll really be glad. Now, review what you've learned in this part of the book. You've mastered the controls. Here are some things you've learned:

- ☞ Access keystrokes require **Alt** followed by another character.

- ☞ Specify access keys for Command Button controls by inserting an ampersand (**&**) before the access key letter in the caption.

- ☞ You can indirectly add access keys for text boxes, but you must add the access key to the Label control that describes the text box. When the user presses the label's access key, focus can jump to the text box.

A page is a terrible thing to waste.

Part III
I've Got to Learn a New Language?

This part of the book teaches you a new language. Rest assured, however, that the new language isn't as difficult as the foreign language you took in high school. Visual Basic uses all sorts of common, everyday words—not exactly the way you're used to speaking them—but several words are close.

You'll see how Visual Basic can do math, store data, and repeat things over and over without getting bored.

Be warned: Although you'll enjoy this part's material, it will not be as hands-on as the material in the previous chapters. You've got to learn a few Visual Basic language commands and requirements so you can add the VB language to your forms and programs to make them extremely powerful. No matter how much you can do with a form and controls, your programming power increases dramatically when you learn a few words of the Visual Basic language.

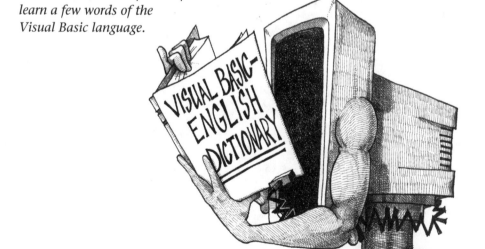

Chapter 14

Variables Don't Stay the Same

In This Chapter

☛ Using variables

☛ Declaring variables

☛ Understanding variable data types

The first place to begin any programming language is learning how that language stores data. You've already seen some vehicles that hold data; one example is the Text property in Text Box controls. In a way, the Caption properties of Label and Command Button controls also hold data (the name that appears on the Label and Command Button controls).

There comes a time when such data-holding places don't suffice for all your needs. You've got to have other places to put values. For example, what if you write a program that contains two text boxes, one to hold customer IDs and one for customer purchase amounts. After entering the information for each customer, you want to store those values and display a blank form for the next customer. Where do you store the values? You can store them in memory or on the disk. This chapter discusses the former, in-memory, method.

What Is a Variable?

You know that your computer has memory. As mentioned in this chapter's opening, there are two kinds of memory. Short-term memory holds the work your computer (as well as your program, the operating system, and Windows) is currently processing. Long-term memory, memory that retains its data values long after you switch off your computer, is the disk memory.

TECHNO NERD TEACHES...

Your computer's nondisk memory is sometimes called *RAM*, *dynamic memory*, or just plain *memory*.

To your PC, memory is a lot like your own brain's memory, and the disk memory is a lot like a printed book. The book's data is safely tucked away, but when you want to process the book's contents, you must read the contents into your memory (and some of us have shorter-term memory than others).

When your VB program computes totals or concatenates text, that data must be in the computer's memory.

SPEAK LIKE A GEEK

A *variable* is a named storage place in memory.

Likewise, before you can edit a word-processed letter, or before you can change a form in a program you wrote last week, or before you can print the spreadsheet of last month's tax records, you must load that word processor disk file, that VB program, or that spreadsheet into the computer's memory. Only after that data is in memory can the computer process that data.

You can have a total of many millions of characters of memory. Each memory address, just like a postal box, has a unique number called an *address*. When you store a value, such as a total, in memory, that data goes to a specific address. Figure 14.1 shows how your memory looks.

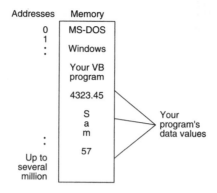

Figure 14.1

Data goes somewhere in memory.

Visual Basic determines exactly what address should store data. Luckily, you never have to mess with actual address numbers. Instead, you can assign names to data and remember only those names. Even though **Text1.Text** is not an extremely descriptive name, you know (after the last few chapters) that **Text1.Text** is the holding place for the first text box label's data. You can change the name of the Text Box control if you like. When you refer to the name, VB looks in an internal table and finds the address of that control's data.

Here's a good use for a variable: Suppose your program contains five text boxes for the previous work week's sales totals, and you must calculate the total sales and display that total. A variable is a perfect place for the total.

If you need more memory storage locations than the controls provide—and you often do need more—you can tell Visual Basic to create one or more variables. When you request a variable, you must do so with VB code.

Requesting that Visual Basic create variables is called *defining* or *declaring* variables.

There's not a hard and fast rule as to when you need a variable. Suffice it to say, however, that most programs that do a lot of work need variables. You'll pick up the *why* and *when* of variables as you progress through VB programming.

Don't type the brackets! In a statement's format, the brackets indicate optional parts of the statement. You don't have to specify a type, but you probably should.

Therefore, if you need an extra storage place for a control's value, you'll first define a variable to hold the data.

Defining Variables

Whereas disk files have filenames, variables have variable names. You must supply the name when you define the variable. Although VB is lenient with the names you give variables, you must follow these simple rules (you'll also need to follow these naming rules when naming the subroutines and functions that you write):

☛ A variable name can range from 1 to 40 characters

☛ A variable name must begin with a letter

☛ After the first letter, your variable name can contain letters, numbers, and the underscore character

☛ You cannot give a variable the same name as a reserved word (a VB command)

These are great variable names:

Total
Sales94
Feb1994Balance
Gross_Sales

These aren't so good:

#Total
94Sales
Feb-1994-Balance
Gross Sales

You'll use the **Dim** statement to declare variables. Here is the format of the **Dim** statement:

Dim variableName [As *Type*]

A variable's *type* or *data type* tells VB what kind of data the variable will hold.

Table 14.1 lists Visual Basic's data types. These data types can follow the **As** keyword. The first five data types are numeric. If you declare a variable to be a numeric variable, you can then store only numbers. (If you hated high school math, check out the table's Description column, which tells what each data type means.) The sixth data type can hold date and time values. The final data type can hold text values.

A variable is somewhat like a named box in memory. You put things (data values) in the box. The contents of the variable determine what type the variable is to be.

Table 14.1   Data Types That Variables Can Hold

Data Type	Sample Values	Description
Integer	-2, 982	Whole numbers that don't have decimal points. An **Integer** has a limited range (from -32768 to 32767).
Long	683123	**Long** variables take more memory than regular **Integer** variables, but they can hold much more extreme (larger and smaller) values.
Single	0.3, -88.6	Numbers that contain decimal points (accurate to 6 decimal places).
Double	-433.4455	Numbers that contain decimal points (accurate to 14 decimal places). These are useful for scientific and high-precision mathematics.
Currency	755.22	Values that remain accurate to 2 decimal places. These are useful for currency values (no kidding!).

continues

Table 14.1   Continued

Data Type	Sample Values	Description
Date/Time	12/05/96	Stores date and, optionally, time values in several formats.
String	"Text"	Any non-numeric text, including letters, digits not used in calculations (such as phone numbers), and special characters, in any combination.
Variant	*Anything*	A **Variant** variable can hold any kind of data. The **Variant** can be useful, but it also can lead to sloppy programming. Define variables of specific data types right now, and you'll see later how to use **Variants**.

When making up variable names, use meaningful variable names. If you wanted to store point values for a soccer team, you could use **p** as a valid variable name, but **PointValues** is a much more descriptive name.

Keep the case of variable names constant. If you start a variable with an initial uppercase letter and keep the rest of the name in lowercase, stay with that same case every time you use the variable. If you don't, Visual Basic takes on the nasty habit of changing the case of all variables to the most recent one you typed. Therefore, if you capitalized **Sales** throughout a long subroutine, and then toward the end you used **sales**, forgetting the uppercase letter, Visual Basic would change all your occurrences of **Sales** to **sales**, even though that's not what you intended.

Sample Declarations

To wrap up this chapter, you'll now see some variable declarations. Keep in mind the following:

☞ You declare variables in code, not on a form, control, or by using properties.

☞ You should declare all variables with **Dim** before you use them. This isn't a strict VB requirement, but you'll be better off now if you get in the habit of declaring all variables.

☞ You'll use variables in calculations and for temporary storage of data values before sending those values to the disk.

☞ You'll see in the next chapter how to put values in variables. For now, concentrate on declaring variables.

Suppose that you wanted to declare a variable to hold the week of sales figures described earlier. A **Currency** variable would work just fine. Therefore, the following statement declares a variable named **SaleTotal**:

Dim SaleTotal As Currency

Suppose that you needed to declare a variable that will hold someone's age. This statement will declare an integer variable named **age**:

Dim age As Integer

Suppose that you wanted to keep track of exact temperature readings in a variable. This statement will declare such a variable:

Dim Temp As Single

Imagine that you are helping a scientist friend with an atom analyzer, and the scientist requires highly accurate precision. The following statement declares a variable named **Reading** that can hold high-precision data:

Dim Reading As Double

Don't over-declare a variable. In other words, don't use a **Long** variable when a regular **Integer** variable will hold your data. Don't declare a **Double** variable when a **Single** variable will hold your data. The larger data types consume twice the memory and take longer to process.

String is a computer term for zero or more characters (letters, digits, or special characters such as *, &, and $) strung together and taken as a whole chunk; for example, a name, address, or city name.

If you need a **Variant** variable, you don't have to specify the **As Variant** part of the **Dim** statement. The following statement is identical to the previous declaration:

Dim *anything*

Generally, you'll know in advance what kind of data a variable will hold. If you need a variable that will hold titles of books, you'd need to declare a **String** variable like this:

Dim Title As String

In those rare instances when you need a variable and you can't predict exactly what data it will hold, declare a **Variant** variable:

Dim anything As Variant

The Least You Need to Know

This has been the least hands-on chapter you've read in a while. Nevertheless, it is vital that you get this background under your belt. You probably have lots of questions about variables. The most important thing you should know about variables at this time is how to declare them. You also need to know the difference between the data types. The types are critical; if you declare an **Integer** variable, don't put a number such as **56.543** in that variable, or Visual Basic will ignore the portion of the number to the right of the decimal point (remember, integers cannot hold partial values). Here are some highlights you should remember:

- ☞ Know the difference between nondisk memory and disk memory.

- ☞ Disk data must be read into memory before your computer can process that data.

- ☞ Variables are short-term holding places for data, and you'll use variables to store valuable data that you've calculated and obtained from the user.

- ☞ You should use the **Dim** statement to declare variables so that VB can keep track of the variable data types.

Chapter 15

Putting Stuff in Variables

In This Chapter

- ☞ Using the assignment to store values in variables
- ☞ Storing **String** values using quotation marks around the text string being assigned
- ☞ Assigning variables with the help of **Chr()**
- ☞ Holding **Variant** variables with **Empty** until you store something in them

Now that you know how to declare variables, you need to put stuff *in* those variables! This is the easy part. You use something you already know: the assignment statement. After you get a foothold in this short chapter, Chapter 16, "Doing Math," shows you how to let Visual Basic do your math homework using variables and math operators.

Number Assignments

Use the assignment statement to store values in variables. For instance, if you wanted to store the value **85.7** in a variable named **Average**, you would use this assignment statement:

Average = 85.7

Remember, the assignment statement takes whatever is on the right of the equals sign and stores that value in the object on the left. In the case of variables, the *object* is just a variable name. Be sure that you've declared the variable before you assign a value to it.

Procedure is a general name for both a function and a subroutine.

Visual Basic stores a **0** (or **0.0**, depending on the type) in all numeric variables you declare with **Dim**. The variable holds the zero until you store another value in the variable.

The variable named **Average** now holds a value of **85.7**. The **85.7** value stays in **Average**, just as if **Average** were a box holding something, until you put something *else* in **Average**, or until the function or subroutine ends.

When the procedure with the **Dim** statement that declares a variable ends, that variable goes away. The lifetime of such a variable is short, and the variable is known as a *local variable* because that variable is known locally within that procedure but not within other procedures.

When it becomes important, you'll see how to declare variables known across more than one procedure. Using **Dim** means that two or more procedures can use the same variable name but the name really refers to different variables. Be careful when naming variables—try not to duplicate names among procedures unless the variable is declared in such a way as to be known in more than one procedure.

If the following statement appeared in the procedure a few statements after the previous assignment statement, **Average** would no longer hold **85.7**, but **99.6**:

Average = 99.6

You can store the contents of one variable in another. For example, the next assignment statement takes the value stored in **Average**, and assigns that value to **newAverage**:

    newAverage = Average

After this assignment, the **Average** variable still holds its value. Only the left-hand side of an assignment changes.

TECHNO NERD TEACHES...

You can store more in variables than just values and other variables. You'll see in the next chapter how to store in variables the results of mathematic equations.

You can also store the contents of controls in variables. This is where the **Variant** comes in handy, because controls don't have specific data types as variables do. Therefore, if **Anything** is declared as a **Variant** variable, the following assignment statement stores the contents of the first Text Box control (entered by the user) in **Anything**:

Anything = Text1.Text

String Variables

When you store a value in a string variable, you must put that value inside quotation marks. For example, to put the string **Bill Gates** into the **String** variable named **King**, you'd do this:

    King = "Bill Gates"

The quotation marks are *not* stored in the variable. The variable named **King** now holds **Bill Gates**. You'll use **String** variables to hold any data that you'll *not* do math with. For example, phone numbers and Social Security Numbers are numeric digits, but because you never do math with such values, you can store them in **String** variables.

There is a way to store quotation marks in a **String** variable. To do so, you must revisit the **Chr()** function you learned earlier in the book. Remember that the argument you give to **Chr()** must be a number from the ASCII table (see Appendix A, "ASCII Table"). The ASCII table holds the quotation mark character at ASCII value 34. Suppose you wanted to put the string **He said, "I quit!"** in a **String** variable. By using **Chr()** and the concatenation sign, you can do it like this:

Sentence = "He said, " + Chr(34) + "I quit!" + Chr(34)

Keep things balanced! Don't put text in a numeric variable, and don't put a number in a **String** variable.

Notice that each small string within the concatenated parts must be enclosed in quotation marks. The **Chr(34)** becomes the quotation mark character when concatenated to the rest of the strings.

If you store a string in a **Variant** variable, you must also enclose the string inside quotation marks. When you assign a **Variant** variable a numeric value, of course you don't use the quotation marks around the number.

Whereas numeric variables start off with a zero value, **String** variables start off with the *null string*. Null strings are often represented by two side-by-side quotation marks, like this: *""*. When a **String** variable contains the null string, that **String** variable is assumed to have no string in it.

Special Variant Values

Although I warned you against using **Variant**, I keep coming back to it, don't I? Actually, the *real* rule is don't use **Variant** when you know the kind of data that a variable will hold. Nevertheless, there are two values that a **Variant** variable can hold that other variables cannot.

From the time you declare a **Variant** variable until you assign something to it, the **Variant** holds the special value called **Empty**. Later, you'll learn how to test variables for values. You can even test a **Variant** variable for the **Empty** value.

If you assign zero or a null string to a **Variant** variable, the **Variant** will no longer be considered to be **Empty**, and you cannot successfully test for the **Empty** value.

Sometimes, especially when working with large amounts of disk data, you'll want to indicate that a value is missing from the data. You can assign the **Null** value to **Variant** variables to indicate that there is missing data and that you would assign something (replacing the **Empty** value) if there were data.

The Least You Need to Know

This is another one of those theory chapters. It's short, to keep your interest. Now, however, you're ready to get back to the keyboard (Yeah!). With the variable tools you've picked up in this and the previous chapter, you're ready to make Visual Basic store math results in variables. These are some things to keep in mind:

- ☞ The assignment statement puts values into variables.

- ☞ A variable declared with **Dim** holds its value until you assign something else in it or until the procedure ends.

- ☞ You can store in variables values, control values, or other variable contents.

- ☞ You need to put quotation marks around text strings when you store the text in **String** variables.

- ☞ A **Empty** value means that a **Variant** variable has yet to be assigned a value.

- ☞ An **Null** value means that a **Variant** variable would have been assigned something, but the data was missing.

Here's that blank page thing again.

Chapter 16
Doing Math

In This Chapter

☛ Learn the math operators

☛ Watch out for the math calculating priority

☛ Use **Val( )** to convert **String** values to numbers

Turn VB into a calculator! On second thought, it's a lot easier just to buy one of those $10 solar jobbies. Nevertheless, Visual Basic can perform lots of math calculations, and you'll need those calculations for the applications that you write.

To calculate, you only need to know how to use the math operators. The math operators explained in this chapter (the only ones you use the majority of the time) look and act a lot like their counterparts on a calculator keypad.

An *operator* is a symbol, such as the plus sign, that does mathematic work.

The **&** works as a concatenation operator, just as **+** does. If you don't want **+** doing two jobs, use **&** for concatenation and **+** for math. It's a matter of style. Microsoft recommends using **&** (what do *they* know?).

Back to Basics: Primary Math

Table 16.1 lists the four primary Visual Basic math operators. See, I told you they are familiar. You've seen the plus sign used already, haven't you? The plus sign has two purposes: to concatenate strings and to add numeric values. If you put strings on each side of **+**, VB knows to concatenate. If you put numbers on each side, Visual Basic adds the numbers.

Table 16.1   The Primary Math Operators

Operator	Function
+	Addition
-	Subtraction
*	Multiplication
/	Division

You'll use the math operators in assignment statements. The results of the math go into the variable or control that you list on the left of the equals sign. For example, the following statement stores the total of five daily variables in a variable named **Total**:

Total = Day1 + Day2 + Day3 + Day4 + Day5

Obviously, the five daily variables must have been initialized with values before this assignment, or VB would add a bunch of zeros.

The following statement subtracts the cost of sales from the gross sales to produce a net sales value:

NetSales = Sales - CostOfSales

The following statement multiplies a factor by a grand total, and then doubles it:

AdjTotal = Factor * GrandTotal * 2

The following statement divides the grand total by the factor:

AdjTotal = GrandTotal / Factor

If you mix operators, VB has a nasty habit of calculating out of order. VB always calculates multiplication and division before any addition and subtraction. In the assignment

value = 4 + 6 * 2

VB stores **16**, not **20**, in **value**. VB computes the **6 * 2** before adding the product, **12**, to the **4**. It doesn't matter that the addition appears to the left of the multiplication. If the * were a /, VB would compute the addition last because * and / both have priority over +.

If your expression contains a mixture of both * and /, neither has priority over the other, so VB calculates from left to right. Therefore, VB computes the following expression's / before the *:

value = 8 / 2 * 3

VB also computes + and - from left to right if both appear in an expression.

If you want to ensure an exact calculation order, or override the calculation priorities, use parentheses. The parentheses in the following expression ensure that the addition computes before the multiplication:

value = (4 + 6) * 2

VB stores **20** in **value** because the addition is computed before the multiplication occurs.

Put It to Work

Practice using the operators by creating a simple calculator program. Although the calculator program supplied with Windows (look in the Main program group for it) is a lot more powerful, this example demonstrates the math operators extremely well.

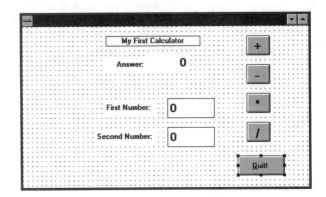

Figure 16.1

A simple calculator.

Using the Operators

Don't forget that controls such as Text Box controls contain values. The Text Box control contains the user's input stored in the Text property. You can combine those values with operators to calculate values.

Create a new application (select New from the File menu) and display the blank form. Add the command buttons, labels, and text boxes shown in Figure 16.1. (The Text Box controls appear to the right of the labels **First Number:** and **Second Number:**).

Add the code for the command button labeled **Quit!**. You don't need help here. Remember, double-click on the command button and add the **End** statement to the body of the **Command5_Click()** subroutine.

You'll now need to add code to the top four command buttons so they perform the calculations needed. Perhaps you've now gathered that this is the goal of the application: VB should take whatever two values appear in the Text Box controls (if the user has not entered anything, the zeros will have to suffice) and perform whatever math the user specifies by clicking the appropriate operator command button. The answer will appear in the Label control next to the **Answer:** label.

BY THE WAY

The FontSize property for the four command buttons, the answer label, and the two text boxes is **13.5**. Right justify the Alignment property of the answer label to the right of **Answer:**. Specify that the Caption property be **0** and specify that the Text property for the two Text Box controls be **0**, as well. Also, to aid your data entry, change the TabIndex property of the first Text Box control to **0** and the second Text Box control to **1**. This ensures that the focus appears in these controls first and second, so the user can start the application and enter the two numbers without having to tab to those numbers first.

The Label control next to **Answer:** probably has the Name property **Label3**. The name depends on the order in which you created the form. If that Label control was not the third item you placed on the form, yours will have a different Name property. Whatever Name property it has (highlight the label and press **F4** to display its Properties window), change the Name property to **lblAnswer**. When you rename a Label control, make the first three letters **lbl** so you'll get a clue from the name about what kind of control it is. (It always helps to document things as well as possible, even in relatively easy applications such as these).

While you're at it, go ahead and rename the Name properties for the two numeric data-entry Text Box controls (where the zeros now appear). Name the first Text Box control **txtNum1** and the second **txtNum2**. See how the initial **txt** lets you know that the control is a Text Box control? Sure, you knew that already, but on a form with many controls (and even worse, in an application with more than one form, each with many controls) the names are easier to remember than default names such as **Label9** and **Text14**.

Make it easy to quit. Add an access key (**Alt+Q**) to the **Quit!** command button by changing its Caption property to **&Quit!**.

You'll now see how the new label names affect your program. Double-click the plus sign command button to open the **Command1_Click()** subroutine code window. Type the following for the body of the subroutine:

You can change the answer's label name to make the rest of the application a little easier.

lblAnswer.Caption = txtNum1.Text + txtNum2.Text

You ought to be able to figure this one out in your sleep! The Caption property (the text displayed on a Label control) of the **lblAnswer** label is assigned the Text property value stored in the first user's Text Box control value and the second user's Text Box control value.

If you had not renamed these three controls, here is what the subroutine's body would have looked like:

Label3.Caption = Text1.Text + Text2.Text

Aren't you glad you changed the names of those controls? Again, in a simple application, having new names doesn't help a lot, but the new names do make the code of the four operator command buttons easier to read.

Although you can probably figure out the code for the other three command buttons, don't do anything with them now. Go ahead and run the program and take a peek at what you've got so far. Follow these steps closely to see something unexpected:

17 plus 23 doesn't equal 1723! Something's wrong. Your window should look something like the one in Figure 16.2. We've got to fix this before going any further.

1. Press **F5** to run the program. The text cursor appears before the first number's **0**.

2. Press the **Del** key (meaning *delete*) to delete the default **0** value that appears when you run the program.

3. Type **17**.

4. Press **Tab** to move the focus to the next text box.

5. Type **23**.

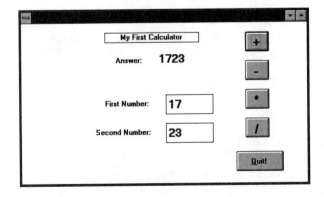

Figure 16.2
17 plus 23 doesn't equal 1723!

6. Now, add the two values and display the result by clicking the plus sign command button.

7. Stop the program's execution by clicking **Quit**.

Fixing the Problem

This is why you learned that the plus sign performs both addition and concatenation before I told you about **&**, which performs only concatenation.

The problem is easy to understand. Visual Basic treats Text Box controls as **String** values. When you "added" the two text box values in the plus sign's **Command1_Click()** subroutine, Visual Basic concatenated what it thought were strings.

You must convert the text box values to numbers before adding their values. There is a Visual Basic function that does just that. The **Val()** function (for *value*) converts its **String** argument to a number. If the value happens not to have a string that converts to a proper number, **Val()** produces a zero result. (In case the user doesn't enter a number, but something else, such as a word.)

Double-click on the plus sign's command button. Modify the body of the subroutine and enclose each side of the + with **Val()**, like this:

lblAnswer.Caption = Val(txtNum1.Text) + Val(txtNum2.Text)

Again run the steps listed at the end of the previous section. As shown in Figure 16.3, the program now works!

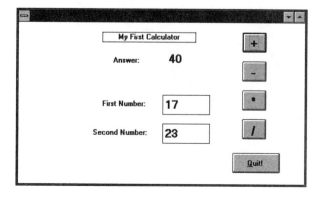

Figure 16.3

17 plus 23 does equal 40. Whew!

Don't leave a **0** in the bottom text box and attempt to divide. You cannot divide by zero. The rules of math don't allow it. Visual Basic will think you're crazy.

More Than Addition

To complete the application, you must add similar code bodies to the remaining three operator command buttons. Assuming that your -, *, and / command buttons are named **Command2**, **Command3**, and **Command4**, respectively, here are the subroutines for the three command buttons:

```
Sub Command2_Click ()
    lblAnswer.Caption = Val(txtNum1.Text) - Val(txtNum2.Text)
End Sub

Sub Command3_Click ()
    lblAnswer.Caption = Val(txtNum1.Text) * Val(txtNum2.Text)
End Sub

Sub Command4_Click ()
    lblAnswer.Caption = Val(txtNum1.Text) / Val(txtNum2.Text)
End Sub
```

Run the program, trying several values and making sure the command buttons work as described. Save the application (select Save from the File menu) as **CALC1.FRM** and **CALC1.MAK** so you can use the form and project again in later chapters.

Put It to Work

I know, you're going to leave the **0** and see what happens, despite the warning. Visual Basic halts the program as soon as you click on the /, giving you a **Division by zero** error. You'll have to press **Enter** to clear the error. Then (Visual Basic makes you pay for your errors) you'll have to select End from the **Run** menu to get back to the program's Design window.

Chapter 19, "**If** True," will show you how to test for the zero and ensure that the user doesn't leave one in the second box. This chapter's application didn't use variables. There was simply no reason to do so.

The Least You Need to Know

You can now make Visual Basic calculate. If the math priorities are giving you trouble, use parentheses to ensure that you get the calculation order you prefer. Visual Basic lets you combine operators, variables, and control values to produce the mathematic answers that you need. Be careful when using control values in expressions because you'll probably have to use **Val( )** to convert the values to numbers. These are a few of this chapter's most important topics:

- ☞ +, -, *, and / perform addition, subtraction, multiplication, and division in VB.

- ☞ VB has a calculation order that you must watch for. Multiplication and division calculate before addition and subtraction if they appear in the same expression.

- ☞ Use **Val( )** to convert control values to numbers that you'll use in expressions. Without **Val( )**, control values remain textual.

What a waste it is to lose one's mind.

Chapter 17
Functions Lighten Your Load

In This Chapter

- ☛ Functions save you work
- ☛ There are numeric and string functions
- ☛ There are functions to convert numbers to integers
- ☛ You can strip off small portions of a longer string

A few built-in functions have been sprinkled here and there throughout this book. This chapter teaches you a few more for your programming bag of tricks. The functions supplied by Visual Basic simply lighten your programming load. You could write code that does virtually everything the functions do. To save you from having to do that, Microsoft supplies many common routines for you.

This is another of those hands-off chapters. You won't see any application here, so you can take a break from your keyboard.

A Function Review

So far, you've learned about these functions:

- ☞ **Chr()**, which converts a number to its matching ASCII character
- ☞ **LCase()**, which converts a **String** value to lowercase
- ☞ **UCase()**, which converts a **String** value to uppercase
- ☞ **Val()**, which converts a **String** value to a number

There are several more. This book doesn't waste your time describing lots of functions you'll rarely use. It concentrates on a few common ones.

Remember that the value you find inside a function's parentheses is called the function argument. In the following assignment statement

    CapName = UCase(LowName)

the **UCase()** argument is **LowName**. In *programming guru* terminology, the argument **LowName** is *passed* to **UCase()**. Some functions can take more than one argument. If a function takes more than one argument, separate the arguments with commas inside the parentheses.

A function *returns* a single value.

There is code behind a function. Someone who worked on the Visual Basic design team wrote the code, so you don't have to. You won't see the code, and that's fine—you don't need or want to. The important thing is that you only have to use the function name and pass the argument that you want the function to work with.

The function call does its job, and then the function's return value replaces the function call in whatever expression uses the function. Consider these two lines:

    MyName = "JILL"
    LowName = LCase(MyName)

In the second statement, **MyName** contains **JILL** and is passed to the **LCase()** function. After **LCase()** does its job, the **LCase(MyName)** function becomes its return value, **jill**.

A function never returns more than one value. If it did, which one of those values would the function call become? Even those few functions that accept more than one argument only return single values. Figure 17.1 shows you that a function is like a magic box that takes one or more arguments, does work with its arguments, and returns a single value.

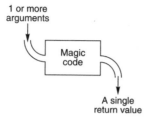

Figure 17.1
A function's job.

Functions are either numeric functions or string functions. The type of function depends on the return value. For example, the **UCase()** function is a string function because the return value is the **String** data type. Usually, the data type of a function's argument (or arguments) matches the return value, but the argument's data type doesn't always match the return value's data type.

Numeric Functions

There are a few helpful math functions that you might need, even in simple applications. Three of these functions convert decimal numbers (of the **Single** or **Double** data types) to integers. You might need to round computed values to whole numbers.

The **Int()** function converts its argument to an integer by returning the closest integer *less than or equal to* the argument. The following assignments assign **1**, **2**, and **3**, respectively:

```
val1 = Int(1.1)
val2 = Int(2.5)
val3 = Int(3.9)
```

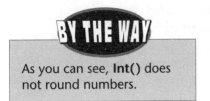

As you can see, **Int()** does not round numbers.

Keep in mind that **Int()** converts its argument to the integer less than or equal to its argument. This is especially critical when you pass negative arguments to **Int()**. The following statements assign -1, -2, and -3, respectively:

```
val1 = Int(-.1)
val2 = Int(-1.5)
val3 = Int(-2.9)
```

The last assignment occurs because **-3** is less than **-2.9**.

If you want the negative values handled differently, use **Fix()**. **Fix()** truncates its argument's decimal portion and returns the integer result. For positive arguments, both **Int()** and **Fix()** return the same value. For negative arguments, **Fix()** simply removes the decimal portion. These three assignments store **0**, **-1**, and **-2** respectively (unlike the previous three, which used **Int()** on the same arguments):

To *truncate* means to chop off and remove.

```
val1 = Fix(-.1)
val2 = Fix(-1.5)
val3 = Fix(-2.9)
```

If you want true rounding in the way you learned in school (rounding .5 or more up to the next integer), use **Cint()** (for *convert integer*). These three assignment statements assign **-6**, **5**, and **6**, respectively:

```
val1 = Cint(-5.9)
val2 = Cint(5.3)
val3 = Cint(5.501)
```

TECHNO NERD TEACHES...

Visual Basic supports lots of trigonometric and scientific functions. Table 17.1 lists some of the most common ones. The trig functions return their values in radians, so if you need the answer in degrees, you'll have to multiply the value by pi (π) and divide by **180**.

Table 17.1 **Trigonometric and Scientific Functions**

Function	Description
Abs( )	Absolute value
Atn( )	Arc tangent
Cos( )	Cosine
Exp( )	Base of the natural logarithm
Log( )	Natural logarithm
Sin( )	Sine
Sqr( )	Square root
Tan( )	Tangent

Some String Functions

In addition to the string functions you've seen, Visual Basic supports a wide variety of other useful string functions. Visual Basic retains the tradition started over a decade ago with Microsoft's first MBASIC language, which contained a wide variety of string functions.

It's time to confess. The string functions described here return a **Variant** data type. If you append a dollar sign, **$**, to the end of these string function names, they'll return the **String** data type.

The **Left( )** and **Right( )** functions each take two arguments. These are considered string functions (despite their **Variant** return values), so they return strings even though one of their arguments is not a string. **Left( )** returns the left portion of a string. The easiest way to learn to use **Left( )** is to see examples. The following statements assign **V**, **Vis**, and **Visual** to the three string variables on the left of the equals signs:

```
part1 = Left("Visual Basic", 1)
vbVar = "Visual Basic"
part2 = Left(vbVar, 3)
part3 = Left(vbVar, 6)
```

Notice that these functions can take a variable or an actual value (known as a *literal* or *constant*).

The **Right()** function is easy to learn now. **Right()** returns the extreme right portion of a string. Take a look at these statements, which store c, sic, and **Basic** in the three variables, **part1**, **part2**, and **part3**:

part1 = Right("Visual Basic", 1)

vbVar = "Visual Basic"

part2 = Right(vbVar, 3)

part3 = Right(vbVar, 5)

If you specify a second argument that's longer than the string argument, VB stores the whole string instead of a partial string.

TECHNO NERD TEACHES...

A *substring* is a portion of a string.

To get the best of both **Left()** and **Right()** worlds, use the **Mid()** function to return any substring from another string. **Mid()** requires *three* arguments. The first argument is the string you want to work on. The second argument is the starting position of the substring you want to strip from the middle of the original string. The third argument is the length of the substring you want to produce.

BY THE WAY

Mid()'s third argument is optional. Without the third argument, **Mid()** returns a substring starting at the position of the second argument and lasting until the end of the original string.

The following assignment stores **al** in the variable named **Part**:

Part = Mid("Visual Basic", 5, 2)

The following assignment stores **Basic** in the variable named **LongPart**. Without the third argument, VB keeps stripping the substring until the end of the original string is reached.

LongPart = Mid("Visual Basic", 8)

Figure 17.2 shows how **Left()**, **Mid()**, and **Right()** operate on the same string.

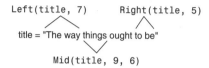

Figure 17.2
The substring functions in action.

The Least You Need to Know

Now you know a few more functions that might save time as you write more Visual Basic code. Some of VB's functions are specific, especially the trigonometric and scientific functions, but others are useful for many things. For example, you might need to strip off the first letter of a user's answer when you ask the user a yes or no question. Once you get the first letter (with **Left()**), you can then convert that letter to uppercase with **UCase()** and test against **Y** to see if the user wants to continue. (You'll learn about data testing in Chapter 19, "If True.") Here are the highlights of VB functions:

- ☞ Functions take arguments and return single values. Never attempt to return more than one value from a function.

- ☞ There are numeric and string functions. The return value's data type determines the function's data type.

- ☞ There are three different kinds of decimal-to-integer conversion functions—**Int()**, **Fix()**, and **Cint()**.

- ☞ The **Left()**, **Mid()**, and **Right()** functions return substrings from longer strings.

This page suitable for doodling.

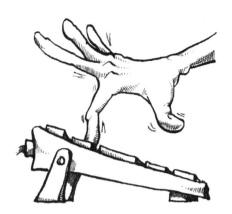

Chapter 18
Input and Output

In This Chapter

- ☛ Learn about VB dialog boxes, called message boxes

- ☛ Determine the difference between the **MsgBox** statement and the **MsgBox()** function (also learn about the parentheses!)

- ☛ Customize a message box message, its title, and the command buttons it displays

- ☛ Use the **InputBox()** function to get answers from the user

You've already performed input and output in Visual Basic programs. Label and Text Box controls make it easy, during design time, to determine exactly what the user will see, and to capture (via the text boxes) what the user enters.

Nevertheless, there are other ways to display information and to capture information typed by the user. Two things that will aid in giving warnings and error messages to the user are input boxes and message boxes. This chapter teaches you all about them.

Input boxes and *message boxes* are pop-up boxes that appear on the screen when input or message output is needed.

Input boxes are dialog boxes that request user input. Message boxes are dialog boxes that display messages to the user.

They're Not Controls

Neither input boxes nor output boxes are controls. They are dialog boxes that display or capture information during the program's running. You've seen dialog boxes before if you've used other Windows applications. A dialog box is a window that appears *over* the user's window.

Dialog boxes don't always appear. In other words, if you need a user's data value every time your program runs, you'll use a Text Box control to grab that data. If, however, you don't always need additional information from the user, depending on the date, data, or a user's previous response to a control, your program can display a dialog box that the user has to respond to before the program will continue.

Figure 18.1 shows an example of a useful message box. Perhaps the user decides to send some information to the printer. The dialog box pops up just to warn the user that the printer must be on and have paper. If, however, the user did not request a printout, the program would have no reason to display this message box information.

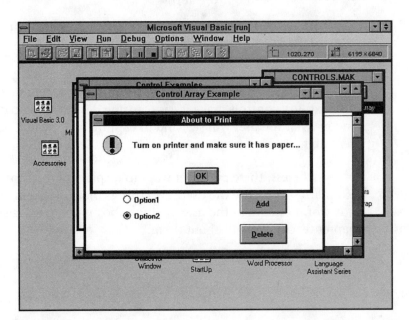

Figure 18.1

A message box prepares the user for printing.

How long should Figure 18.1's message box stay on the screen? As long as the user needs it in order to read the instructions and take needed action. Therefore, even an output-only message box has *some* form of input: The user's **Enter** keypress is needed to clear the message box and let the program continue.

Figure 18.2 shows an input box. Notice that it, as does a message box, contains an **OK** command button so the user can let the program know when to continue. Input boxes also have one or more other command buttons as well as a place for the user to answer a question or type needed text. In Figure 18.2, the user is being asked to enter a password.

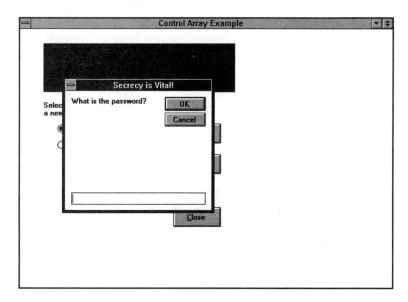

Figure 18.2

An input box asking for a password.

There are several ways to display message boxes and input boxes. The next two sections explain how.

Message Box Usage and Styles

There are actually two kinds of message boxes, although your user won't really know (or care) about the difference between them. One message box is *output only*, meaning that the message box exists solely for displaying a message to the user. The user sees the message until pressing **Enter** to close the message box.

Your program can control the number of command buttons as well as the icon that appears in a message box. For example, Figure 18.1's message box displays a message and a single command button, the **OK** button. You can also display message boxes with **Cancel**, **Yes**, **No**, **Retry**, **Ignore**, and **Abort** buttons. These command buttons are useful for message boxes that ask yes or no questions and ones that give the user a chance to continue with the intended action (such as print a report) by clicking **OK**, or cancel the current operation by selecting the **Cancel** command button.

On an error condition, such as a disk drive not being ready, you can display the **Abort**, **Retry**, or **Ignore** command buttons to see if your user wants to abort the program, retry the disk access, or ignore the error and move on with the program despite potential problems it might cause.

A simple message box requires the **MsgBox** statement. A message box that needs to know the command button pressed requires the **MsgBox()** function. Both the **MsgBox** statement and the **MsgBox()** function accept the same arguments, but the **MsgBox()** function (the only one you can use if you want to know the command button pressed) uses parentheses and the statement does not. Here is the general format of the **MsgBox** statement:

MsgBox msg [,[type][,title]]

Those brackets are confusing. Remember that brackets in program formats indicate the optional pieces of the statement or function. Therefore, the **MsgBox** statement requires a message, followed optionally by a *type* and optionally by a *title*.

Here is the general format of the **MsgBox()** function:

MsgBox(*msg* [,[*type*][,*title*]])

The *msg* argument is whatever string you want displayed in the message's dialog box. The third argument, the *title* argument, is a string that appears in the message box's title bar, across the top of the message box. If you don't specify a title value, VB displays **Microsoft Visual Basic** for the message box title.

Table 18.1 lists the meanings of the *type* argument. The *type* argument requires further explanation, so read on.

Table 18.1   The MsgBox Type Arguments

Value	Meaning
Add a single value from this group:	
0	The **OK** button only
1	The **OK** and **Cancel** buttons
2	The **Abort**, **Retry**, and **Ignore** buttons
3	The **Yes**, **No**, and **Cancel** buttons
4	The **Yes** and **No** buttons only
5	The **Retry** and **Cancel** buttons
To any value in this group:	
16	Display the stop icon
32	Display the question mark icon
48	Display the exclamation point icon
64	Display the lowercase **i** icon (for *information*)
And, optionally, add any value in this group:	
0	The first button has the default focus
256	The second button has the default focus
And, optionally, add any value in this group:	
0	The user's application is *application modal*, meaning that the message box must be handled by the user before the program will continue
4096	The user's application is *system modal*, meaning that the message box must be handled before any other Windows program responds (this is for serious errors the user must handle)

What if you wanted to ask the user a yes or no question in a message box? You'd put this statement in the subroutine you write that displays the message box:

MsgBox "Are you ready?", 4+32, "Question"

The **4** indicates that **Yes** and **No** buttons are desired, and the **32** added to the **4** indicates that the question mark icon displays. The string **Question** will appear in the title bar of the message box. Figure 18.3 shows this message box.

Figure 18.3

A customized message box.

Notice that the **Yes** button has the focus in Figure 18.3. If you wanted **No** to have the default focus, you would add a **256** to the second argument expression (see Table 18.1).

If you want to give the user more than the default one-button **OK** message box, you'll need to know exactly *which* button the user pushed. In the previous **MsgBox** statement, after the message box goes away, the program has no idea which button the user pushed. You must use the **MsgBox()** function for that. Remembering that a function returns a value, here is one way to set up such a **MsgBox()** function call:

PushButton = MsgBox("Are you ready?", 4+32, "Question")

After the user answers the message box, by clicking on either the **Yes** or **No** command button, **PushButton** will contain either **6** or **7**, indicating the user's choice. See Table 18.2 to learn what **6** and **7** mean.

Table 18.2   The MsgBox() Return Value Possibilities

Return Value	Description
1	The user pressed **OK**
2	The user pressed **Cancel**
3	The user pressed **Abort**
4	The user pressed **Retry**
5	The user pressed **Ignore**
6	The user pressed **Yes**
7	The user pressed **No**

If you display a message box with a **Cancel** button, the user can tab to **Cancel**, click **Cancel** with the mouse, or press **Esc** to indicate that **Cancel** is the button of choice.

Input Box Usage and Styles

The **InputBox()** function is virtually identical to the **MsgBox()** function. The difference is that your user can only respond to a fixed number of choices with **MsgBox()** (and those choices are the command buttons that you display), but the user can enter a complete string of text in response to an **InputBox()** message box.

There are actually *two* **InputBox()** functions: **InputBox()** and **InputBox$()**. **InputBox()** (without the dollar sign) returns a **Variant** data type and **InputBox$()** returns a **String** data type. The one you use depends only on the receiving variable's data type. (The **Variant** is more general and is used the most, even though VB programmers almost always store the **InputBox()** return value in a **String** variable.)

Here is the general format of **InputBox()**:

   InputBox(*prompt* [, [*title*][,[*default*][,*xpos, ypos*]]]**)**

Oh boy, those confusing brackets again! The *prompt* is the only thing you *must* specify. Generally, you'll always assign the return value of **InputBox()** to a variable. The *prompt* is the message displayed in the input message box. The *title* is the title bar title, if you want a title (by default, VB doesn't display a title in **InputBox()** message box title bars). The *default* is the string expression displayed for a default answer. You'd use the most common answer to the *prompt* (if there is a common answer, such as a city name), and the user could press **Enter** to select that default or type a new value.

Although not used as much, the *xpos* value indicates the number of twips the left edge of the message box is to appear from the left edge of the screen, and the *ypos* value indicates the number of twips the message box is to appear from the top of the screen.

The following **InputBox( )** function call displays the message box in Figure 18.4.

city = InputBox("What is your city?", "City Ask", "Miami")

Figure 18.4

A message box asking the user for a city name.

If **InputBox( )** returns a null string, "", the user chose **Cancel**.

In Figure 18.4, the city, **Miami**, is the default city. If the user lives in Miami, the user can simply press **Enter** or click **OK** to choose the **OK** button. If the user lives in another city, the user can type that city name in place of **Miami**. As soon as the user chooses **OK**, whatever city appears in the data-entry area at the bottom of the box is stored in the variable named **city**.

The Least You Need to Know

There is little that is difficult with message boxes. You use message boxes to display messages, at runtime, to the user. Often, the message is a warning, reminder, or explanation of an error condition that might have occurred. In Chapter 19, you'll see more functional uses of these message box functions because with Chapter 19's **If** statement, your program will have a mechanism to use for response to message box button clicks and data entry. Here are some message box highlights:

- ☞ Use message boxes to display messages in pop-up dialog boxes.

- ☞ The **MsgBox** statement displays a message and a set of one or more command buttons from which the user can choose.

- ☞ The **MsgBox()** function returns a value indicating the button pressed by the user so your program can determine which button the user pushed.

- ☞ The **InputBox()** function lets the user answer a message box with a typed response, optionally pressing **Enter** to a default text value that your **InputBox()** provides.

Here's that blank page thing again.

Part IV
Control Those Programs!

It's time to take charge! The Visual Basic language is rich in commands, and those commands can really empower you to control what's happening inside VB programs.

The programs that you've seen so far have been nice, but rather passive. You're a take-charge type of person, so you need the tools that will help you charge into the VB language and make programs do what you need them to do.

The last few chapters have been more theory (ugh!) than hands-on. That's okay. It's now time to add a few controlling VB programming language statements to that theory to produce powerful programs that do a lot of work behind the scenes. Building nice, colorful Windows programs is easy. Controlling those programs is easy, too, but it requires a little patience and practice with the VB language.

Perhaps the most important thing that computers can do is test data and make decisions based on that data. That's what you need to learn first. The next chapter explores the all-important If statement, and the four chapters that then follow show variations on program control.

Chapter 19
If True

In This Chapter

- ☞ **If** executes code selectively
- ☞ **If** requires one of these relational operators: <, >, <=, >=, =, or <>
- ☞ **Else** handles false conditions
- ☞ **If** gives you a way to test return values from **MsgBox()** functions

The **If** statement is vital for writing programs that act on the user's response and on data input into the program from the disk. Visual Basic can make decisions based on the result of the **If**. You can instruct VB to follow one of two paths, depending on whether the user presses the **Yes** or **No** command button in a message box.

If: An Overview

Let's get right to work—there's a lot to cover. How would you use the word *if* in day-to-day speech? How about these sentences:

"If I speed, then I'll get a ticket."

"If I make more money, then we'll retire."

The nice thing about **If** is that, despite its slightly rigid format, **If** works just like sentences you speak in everyday life.

Visual Basic's **If** works *just like that!* Well, almost. You have to structure your program's **If** statement to fit this format:

If *relation* **Then**
    One or more VB statements
    End If

When you speak using *if*, the sentence comes in two basic parts. The first part sets up a *relation* that must be true in order for the second part, the *action*, to take place. In the previous sentences, if the first relation, *I speed*, is true, the action, *I'll get a ticket*, will take place. Otherwise, if you don't speed, you won't get a ticket. In the second sentence, *If you make more money*, then and only then *you can retire*. If, however, if you don't make more money, forget the retirement and enjoy many long years of drudgery.

The **If** works in conjunction with **End If**, kind of like **Sub** works in conjunction with **End Sub**.

In the **If** statement's format you can see the *relation*. A Visual Basic relation simply compares two values, whether those values are variables, values, control values, or a combination of any two. You must learn a few new operators, called *relational operators* (sometimes called *conditional operators*), before setting up a relation. Table 19.1 lists the six VB relational operators.

Table 19.1   VB's Relational Operators

Operator	Description	Example
>	Greater than	**If Amount > 40 Then**
<	Less than	**If userAge < 21 Then**
>=	Greater than or equal to	**If txtSales.Text >=** ➥ **20000.00 Then**
<=	Less than or equal to	**If Balance <= 100.00 Then**
=	Equal to	**If button = 1 Then**
<>	Not equal to	**If Answer <> Correct Then**

Often, programmers like to enclose the relation in parentheses. Here is the first line of an **If** statement, with parentheses around the relation:

If (Amount > 40) Then

Indent the body of an **If** statement to separate the body from the rest of the program and make the parts of the **If** statement easier to read.

Using If

The body of an **If** statement only executes if the *relation* bears out to be true. The **If** body can contain one or many statements, and *none* of the statements execute if the *relation* is false. Consider the following lines from a VB program:

```
salary = InputBox("What is your salary?")
If (Salary >= 25000.00) Then
   Taxes = .40 * Salary
   NetPay = Salary - Taxes
End If
ForecastSalary = 1.1 * Salary
```

The user enters a salary value into the **Salary** variable when **InputBox()** displays its message. This code assumes that the programmer declared **salary** earlier in the subroutine. If and only if the salary is more than $25,000 are the taxes and net pay computed. If, however, the user's salary is less than $25,000, *no* taxes or net pay are computed.

It's important for you to realize that the last line, the one that computes **ForecastSalary**, is *always executed*, no matter what the value of **Salary** is. Only the body of the **If**, not any other part of the program, is affected by the condition's true or false comparison. Figure 19.1 helps explain the maybe-execute/maybe-not-execute aspect of **If**.

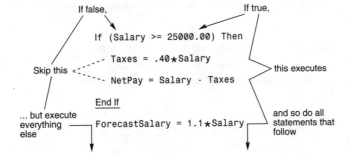

Figure 19.1

If's body may or may not execute.

Here is a section of code that uses a **MsgBox** statement and a **MsgBox()** function. Remember, the **MsgBox()** function returns a value based on the command button clicked by the user. If the user clicks the **Yes** button, a congratulatory message displays.

```
Dim Push As Integer
    Push = MsgBox("Did you win the prize?", 4 + 32, "Win?")
    If (Push = 6) Then
        MsgBox "Congratulations! You're #1!!!", 48, "Yea!"
    End If
```

If you were to put this code in a subroutine that is part of a contest entrant program, Figure 19.2 shows the message box first displayed. If the user clicks on the **Yes** button, the message box in Figure 19.3 displays. If, however, the user clicked **No**, then no extra message box displays, and the program picks up at any statements that follow the **End If**.

Figure 19.2

This message box always displays.

Figure 19.3

This message box displays only if the user presses **Yes**.

Else Handles False Conditions

The **If** statement, as you now know it, decides what code executes if the relation is true. What, however, if there was a second choice? What if you want one set of instructions to execute if the relation is true and another set of instructions to execute if the relation is *false*? The **Else** statement offers an extension of **If**. With **Else**, **If** handles two conditions: a true and a false relation.

When speaking of an **If** combined with **Else** statement, the group is known as the **If-Else** statement.

Here is the format of the **If-Else** statement:

> **If** *relation* **Then**
>   *One or more VB statements*
> **Else**
>   *One or more VB statements*
> **End If**

If the *relation* is true, the first body of statements executes. If, however, the *relation* is false, the second body of statements executes. No matter what the *relation* is, true or false, following **End If** the program resumes execution.

Here is a rewrite of the previous section's **If**. Instead of displaying an extra message box only if the user presses **Yes**, another message box displays if the user presses **No**:

```
Dim Push As Integer
Push = MsgBox("Did you win the prize?", 4 + 32, "Win?")
If (Push = 6) Then
  MsgBox "Congratulations! You're #1!!!", 48, "Yea!"
Else
  MsgBox "I'm sorry, better luck next year.", 48, "Too bad."
End If
```

Of course, **If** statements don't have to have anything to do with message boxes, even though many examples in this chapter have used message boxes. The following **If-Else** computes a bonus if the salesperson sold more than $50,000 worth of goods. If the salesperson didn't meet the quota, there is no bonus. Either way, **Bonus** is assigned the correct value.

```
If (Sales > 50000.00) Then
    Bonus = 75.00
Else
    Bonus = 0.0
End If
```

Okay, now for a little pop quiz. What program do you think the following code will help you with?

```
Sub Command4_Click ()
  If (Val(txtNum2.Text) = 0) Then
    MsgBox "I can't divide by zero!", 0 + 48
  Else
    lblAnswer.Caption = Val(txtNum1.Text) / Val(txtNum2.Text)
  End If
End Sub
```

Do you recognize some of the code? At the end of Chapter 16, "Doing Math," you saw a calculator program that could cause trouble if the user divided by zero. An **If**, however, testing for the zero *before* the division is done, ensures that the division and the subsequent error will never happen. If the user attempts to divide by zero, this code won't let the user divide. When the user presses the **OK** button, the calculator redisplays and awaits a more valid request from the user. This simple **If** keeps the abortive "Division by zero" error from appearing.

The Least You Need to Know

The **If** statement is easy to use because **If** lets your code make decisions that work a lot like the decisions you make in everyday life. The **If** relation operators compare data. When you compare two values, the first value is either more, less, equal to, not equal to, greater than or equal to, or less than or equal to the other value. There are simply no more choices. **If** lets you control which parts of your program execute based on the results of relational testing. Here are some of this chapter's most important highlights:

- ☞ **If** lets your program make decisions based on the values in variables and the result of relational tests.

- ☞ **If** requires a knowledge of the relational operators so you can compare data.

- ☞ The **If** *relation* statement produces a true or false result and the program acts accordingly.

- ☞ **Else** gives **If** more power. The **If** determines the code that executes if the *relation* is true, and the **Else** determines the code that executes if the *relation* is false.

**If this were the last chapter,
you'd be done by now.**

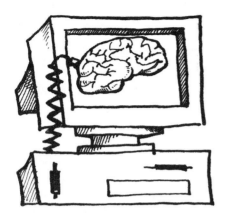

Chapter 20
Select a Case

In This Chapter

- Use **Select Case** to handle multiple choices
- Add **Case Else** to expect the unexpected
- Replace many-layered **If-Else** statements with simpler **Select Case** statements

Do you like multiple-choice tests better than essay tests? Most people do. So does Visual Basic. The **Select Case** is Visual Basic's vehicle for selecting from a list of choices. In a way, the **Select Case** is like an **If** statement that has more than two (true and false) possible outcomes. If your program must choose one of two possible outcomes, nothing beats **If**. If your program must choose one of many different outcomes, **Select Case** wins the honors for *most-helpful statement*.

The Format of Select Case

The format of **Select Case** looks foreboding. Hold your breath, because here it comes:

> **Select Case** *expression*
> **Case** *value*
>   *One or more VB statements*
> **Case** *value*
>   *One or more VB statements*
> [**Case** *value*
>   *One or more VB statements*]
> [**Case Else**
>   *One or more VB statements*]
> **End Select**

The *value* must be a **String** or **Integer** data type. The block of code that executes depends on which *value* matches the *expression*.

Look at the message box displayed in Figure 20.1. The user may press any one of the three command buttons. The command button pressed determines what the rest of the program is to do. As you can imagine, the programmer has to write three different routines, and only one of those three routines will execute depending on the result of the user's button press.

Figure 20.1

A message box with three command buttons.

Here are the three possible return values from this message box: **3** for the **Abort** button, **4** for the **Retry** button, and **5** for the **Ignore** button. (Chapter 18, "Input and Output," explains these return values more fully.)

The **Select Case** statement can check for these three return values. Here is a simple **Select Case** that would handle the three return values (assume the program had assigned the **MsgBox( )** function's return value to a variable named **HandleIt**):

```
Select Case HandleIt
Case 3:
   AbortFunction( )
Case 4:
   RetryDiskRead( )
Case 5:
   ContinueFunction( )
End Select
```

Here is what this **Select Case** statement is saying in Visual Basic speak:

The **Select Case** statement takes the place of the following set of **If-Else** statements, only you've got to admit that the **Select Case** statement is easier to follow!

```
If (HandleIt = 3) Then
   AbortFunction( )
Else If (HandleIt = 4) Then
   RetryDiskRead( )
   Else If (HandleIt = 5)
Then
      ContinueFunction( )
   End If
End If
```

*"If the variable named **HandleIt** contains a 3, then I must execute the **AbortFunction( )** procedure. If the variable named **HandleIt** contains a 4, then I must execute the **RetryDiskRead( )** procedure. If the variable named **HandleIt** contains a 5, then I must execute the **ContinueFunction( )** procedure."*

Looking More Deeply into the Select Case Statement

The **Select Case** statement in the previous example should be fairly easy to understand. It must appear after the **MsgBox( )** function assigns its return value to the **HandleIt** variable. Somewhere at the top of the procedure, the **HandleIt** variable should have been declared with **Dim**.

Functions or subroutines execute if **HandleIt** contains a **3**, **4**, or **5**. These functions that execute are, however, not functions or subroutines that are built into Visual Basic. Therefore, what are **AbortFunction( )**, **RetryDiskRead( )**, and **ContinueFunction( )**?

These are *user-defined functions*. The name *user-defined* is a little misleading because the user doesn't define them—you, the programmer, define them. (Many times, though, you are your own user.) In the previous **Select Case** statement, instead of inserting many lines of code for each **Case** block, the programmer stuck each set of **Case** code in functions that the programmer wrote, called **AbortFunction( )**, **RetryDiskRead( )**, and **ContinueFunction( )**.

Don't worry too much about user-defined functions at this point. However, keep in mind that when you see a function name (always with parentheses) that is not a built-in VB function, the programmer wrote the code and placed that code in a procedure not unlike the **Command1_Click( )** and other procedures you've written in this book.

As a programmer, you can define your own subroutines as well as functions.

Instead of being *event driven*, that is, instead of executing when triggered by an event (such as a mouse click) that happens during the program's execution, user-defined functions are always *called* by name from another procedure somewhere. In the previous **Select Case** statement, the user-defined function is called if its matching **Case** statement executes.

More Select Case Insight

The **MsgBox( )** function is built-in, and you can always count on it returning one of the values promised. However, you cannot always count on the user entering correct values or answering your questions correctly.

For example, suppose that you wanted to ask the user a yes or no question using an **InputBox( )** function. Figure 20.2 shows an input message box triggered by this assignment statement:

> **userAns = InputBox("Are you ready to print (Y/N)?", "Print?",**
> ➥ **"Y")**

Figure 20.2

An input message box asking a yes or no question.

As you can see, the default answer is **Y**. The user might type an **N**, or actually type a full word such as **Yes, YES, no, nO,** or virtually any combination of yes or no answers. Even worse, the user might not even enter an expected answer. The user could enter something like **I am.**

Therefore, when testing for possible values, especially when testing for a user's input, you must expect the unexpected. That's what the **Case Else** statement is all about.

The **Case Else** takes control when none of the other **Case** options match the **Select Case** variable.

Consider the following section of code, which triggers and then handles Figure 20.2's input message box:

```
Dim userAns As String
userAns = InputBox("Are you ready to print (Y/N)?", "Print?", "Y")
userAns = Left(userAns, 1)
userAns = UCase(userAns)
Select Case userAns
   Case "Y" :
     printRoutine( )
   Case "N" :
     processRoutine( )
   Case Else :
     MsgBox "Yikes! You didn't answer Y or N...", 0+16
     End
End Select
```

As soon as the user answers the **InputBox( )** function, the program changes the value entered in the **userAns** string. Whenever you see the same variable on both sides of an equals sign, the variable is being changed. Its old value (on the right of the equals sign) is changed, and then stored in the variable on the left of the equals sign. The assignment right after the **InputBox( )** function stores the first letter of whatever the user entered in **userAns**. The program then, on the next statement, converts that letter to its uppercase equivalent (in case the user didn't type in uppercase). Then, and only then, can the **Select Case** test against an uppercase **Y** and an uppercase **N**.

The **Case Else** statement handles the rare but possible situation where the user doesn't enter anything that starts with **Y** or **N**. The message box displayed by the **Case Else** code ensures that the user knows the problem before the program terminates execution.

The Least You Need to Know

The **Select Case** statement is a lot like a multiple-choice **If-Else** statement. Whereas **If-Else** handles only two possibilities, **Select Case** handles more than two. You can use several layers of **If-Else** in place of **Select Case**, but **Select Case** is a lot easier to read and write. When you have to change a program later, because of changing business practices or whatever, you'll find that it's a lot easier to decipher **Select Case** statements than to wade through layers of **If-Else**. The following list explains the most important aspects of **If-Else**:

- **Select Case** chooses from several possible outcomes, and you'll find **Select Case** easier to use than **If-Else**.

- One or more statements can appear after a **Case** statement. Each statement represents a possible outcome.

- You can write your own subroutine and function procedures if you want to group important and often-needed sections of code together.

- The **Case Else** statement handles unexpected choices. Always include **Case Else** if you want to handle all possibilities.

Chapter 21
Do a Loop

In This Chapter

- Loops are sections of code that repeat over and over and over and over and over...

- The logical operators **And** and **Or** give power to loops

- Loops test relational conditions just as the **If** statement does

You can use Visual Basic to make decisions. Decision making, with **If** and **Select Case** types of statements, is a vital element of programming languages. Repetition comprises just as important a part of any computer language. Computers do not get bored. Computers are better than people at repeating the same tasks over and over.

The programs that you've seen so far haven't needed loops, and not every program you write in the future will need loops. Nevertheless, you've got to learn about loops for those times when you *do* need the repetition they provide. There are several ways to loop in Visual Basic. This chapter teaches you about one kind of loop, and Chapter 22, "Loop **For** as Long as You Need," explains another.

The Do Loop

The two most common **Do** loops are the **Do While-Loop** and the **Do-Loop While** loops. The dashes in the names **Do While-Loop** and **Do-Loop While** indicate where the bodies of the loops go. Here is the statement format of the **Do While-Loop** loop:

> **Do While** *relation*
>   *One or more VB statements*
> **Loop**

Here is the statement format of the **Do-Loop While** loop:

> **Do**
>   *One or more VB statements*
> **Loop While** *relation*

A **Do** loop continues executing as long as the *relation* is true. You learned about relation testing in Chapter 19, "**If** True." A *relation* in Visual Basic is any data testing that's done using any of the six relational operators, such as < and >=. You know that a *relation* is either true or false. If it is true, a **Do** loop keeps executing.

An **If** statement executes its body of code one time, at most, depending on the result of the *relation*. A **Do** loop executes its body of code one or more times, depending on the result of *relation*.

An *iteration* is a single execution of a loop's body of code. If the body of a loop executes three times, three iterations are said to have occurred.

The primary difference between the two **Do** loops is the placement of the *relation*. The **Do While-Loop** executes zero or more times because Visual Basic tests the *relation* before it tests the loop body. The **Do-Loop While** always executes its body at least one time because Visual Basic does not test the *relation* until the body of the loop executes the first time.

Compound Relations

One kind of compound relation is when you're trying to describe how your second cousin's wife's mother's brother-in-law is related to you, but we're not talking about that kind of compound relation here. In computer terms, a *compound relation* is simply two or more relational tests strung together. Although compound relations are possible to form using the **If** statement, compound relations are almost always needed in **Do** loop relational tests. Therefore, let's hold off on loops just for a moment while you learn about compound relational tests.

There are many times when the simple relational operators won't suffice by themselves. What, for instance, if you want to reward someone who has sold more than $5000 worth of goods *or* who has worked more than 50 hours a week (or both)? The following pair of **If** statements would work:

```
If (sales > 5000) Then
  MsgBox "Congratulations on a job well done!"
End If
If (hoursWorked > 50) Then
  MsgBox "Congratulations on a job well done!"
End If
```

Such a double **If** statement will accomplish its goal, but the code is more redundant than it needs to be. You can put two or more relational tests together by using one of the *logical operators* shown in Table 21.1.

Table 21.1   The Logical Operators

Operator	Description
And	Both sides of the **And** must be true for the relation to be true.
Or	Either side of the **Or** must be true for the relation to be true.

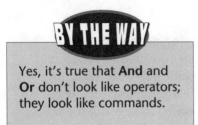

Yes, it's true that **And** and **Or** don't look like operators; they look like commands.

The **And** and **Or** determine how two relations are to be combined into a compound relational test. This one compound **If** is all that's needed to congratulate the aforementioned salesperson:

If (sales > 5000) Or (hoursWorked > 50) Then
    MsgBox "Congratulations on a job well done!"
End If

In spoken text, this is what the **If** says:

"If the sales total more than $5000, or if the hours are more than 50, then congratulate the salesperson."

The primary difference between **And** and **Or** is the strength of the relation needed to form a true condition. In simple terms, **And** is stricter than **Or**. By replacing the previous code's **Or** with an **And**, the salesperson must sell over $5000 and work lots of hours. Here is that **If**:

If (sales > 5000) And (hoursWorked > 50) Then
    MsgBox "Congratulations on a job well done!"
End If

In spoken text, this is what the **If** now says:

"If the sales total more than $5000, and if the hours are more than 50, then and only then congratulate the salesperson."

The **And** says that both relations on each side of the **And** must be true before the **If** tests as true and before the body of the **If** executes.

Show Me a Loop!

Here are the two most common uses for loops in Visual Basic:

- ☞ For input verification to ensure that the user enters expected values

- ☞ In math calculations that require lots of iterations

The following **InputBox( )** function

> **Dept = Val(InputBox("Type your department code, either 1 or 2"))**

produces the input message box shown in Figure 21.1.

Figure 21.1

Waiting for the user's department code.

Who's to say that the user will type a correct value? You could test for the value with a **Select Case** statement, as in the following section of code:

```
Dept = Val(InputBox("Type your department code, either 1 or 2"))
Select Case Dept
  Case 1:
    MsgBox "You come to work at 9:00 am"
  Case 2:
    MsgBox "You come to work at 8:00 am"
  Case Else:
    MsgBox "You entered an incorrect department!"
  End
End Select
```

The problem with such verification of user input is that you shouldn't stop a program just because the user made a typing mistake. The best way to handle bad user input is to ask the user *again* for better values. If then user *still* enters bad data, ask again, and so on until the user wises up and actually begins to pay attention!

Remember that a loop is perfect for repeating sections of code. Therefore, anytime you want the user to enter a value that falls within a certain range or set of values, use a loop. If the user does not enter a correct value, the loop makes sure that the user is given another chance to answer correctly.

The following section of code keeps asking the user for a **1** or **2** department code until the user enters a **1** or a **2**:

```
Do
  Dept = Val(InputBox("Type your department code, either 1 or 2"))
Loop While (Dept < 1) Or (Dept > 2)

Select Case Dept
  Case 1:
    MsgBox "You come to work at 9:00 am"
  Case 2:
    MsgBox "You come to work at 8:00 am"
End Select
```

The loop *ensures* that the **Select Case** gets good values. Therefore, you don't need to specify a **Case Else**.

The body of the **Do-Loop While** contains only a single statement in this example, but it could have more, if needed. The loop says the following:

*"Do a user data entry with **InputBox()** and keep looping if the user's answer is less than 1 or more than 2. (The department code* must *be a 1 or a 2, according to the instructions given to the user.)"*

Only after ensuring, with the **Or** operator, that the user entered a correct value does the program continue and test the department with a **Select Case** statement and print an appropriate message.

TECHNO NERD TEACHES...

The body of any loop *must* change the *relation* somehow. If the *relation* is true, the body of the loop executes. If something inside the loop body does not eventually change a variable inside the *relation*, the *relation* will always remain true, and the loop will loop forever!

A forever loop is called an *infinite loop* in computer lingo. If you accidentally get yourself into an infinite loop, select End from the VB **R**un menu, and Visual Basic will regain control. If the VB menus are hidden behind the application's window, double-click the window's control button to close the running application. Then fix the infinite loop as fast as you can!

The Other Loop

The previous section explains the **Do-Loop While**. Remember, that loop is useful when you want the body of the loop to execute at least once. The user had to be asked the question, and the question appeared inside the body of the loop. Therefore, the **Do-Loop While** worked great. This section shows you a variation called the **Do While-Loop**.

Another common use of loops is to calculate math iterations. If you don't like math, that's fine—you don't have to be a pro to use loops. For example, most math is composed of a bunch of fun puzzles (not your idea of *fun*, eh?). Can you spot a pattern in the following numbers?

1 1 2 3 5 8 13 21 34 55 89

Take each pair of numbers, from left to right, and add them together. You'll get the next number in the sequence. 1+1=2, 1+2=3, 2+3=5, 3+5=8, and so on. This number pattern in called the *Fibonacci sequence*, patterned after the great Italian Renaissance mathematician Fibonacci somebody. (I believe that he also played for the Jets in '68, but I'm not sure.)

The Fibonacci sequence has practical purposes. The sequence appears throughout nature. Count petals on many roses, and the petals form the Fibonacci sequence. The Fibonacci sequence is also used a lot in probability theory to aid in gambling predictions (I just *knew* I'd get your attention!).

Enough about Fibonacci. Using a **Do While-Loop**, you can print a sequence of numbers up to a value entered by the user. The following code is the longest set of code that you've seen in the book. As you learn more about programming, you'll find many ways to improve it. However, this is a first step toward displaying the Fibonacci sequence to the user, one step at a time, through the use of message boxes.

```
Dim userN As Integer
Dim fib1 As Integer
Dim fib2 As Integer
Dim fib3 As Variant
Do
   userN = Val(InputBox("Type a number (1 to 55) and I'll give you
➥ Fibonacci"))
```

```
Loop While (userN < 1) Or (userN > 55)

fib1 = 1
fib2 = 1
MsgBox ("The next value is 1")
MsgBox ("The next value is 1")
fib3 = fib1 + fib2
Do While (fib3 <= userN)
  fib3 = fib1 + fib2
  MsgBox ("The next value is " + fib3)
  fib1 = fib2
  fib2 = fib3
Loop
End
```

Sure, all those message boxes that display only a single number are cumbersome, but you get the point.

This code uses two **Do** loops. The user is asked for a number, and then a Fibonacci sequence displays up to that number, and possibly one additional Fibonacci number, depending on the user's value. Two **1s** are displayed just to get things started. Then the second **Do** loop ensures that each pair of numbers is added to a third. The third value, **fib3**, is declared as a **Variant** variable because **MsgBox** displays only strings and **MsgBox** converts **fib3** to a string before concatenating **fib3** to the end of the message **The next value is**.

The **Do While (fib3 <= userN)** ensures that the sequence doesn't go too far past the user's input value found in **userN**.

Put It to Work

Don't see how to implement this code? Perhaps this code could be run when the user clicks a command button labeled **Fibonacci**.

The Least You Need to Know

Loops give you computing power that would otherwise be wasted. After you set up a loop, your computer can do all the boring repetitive work while you file your nails. Loops are perfect for verifying user input, and this chapter shows you two loops: the **Do-Loop While** and the **Do While-Loop**. The difference between the **Do** loops is the location of the relational test in each of them.

Unlike an **If** statement, a loop may repeat its body of code many times, as long as the relational test is true. **If** quits after one execution, even if its relational test is still true. Often, the logical operators **And** and **Or** (or is it **And** *or* **Or**? Oh, gosh…) help combine relational tests to give more power to loops. Here are some looping highlights from this chapter:

- ☞ Loops are sections of code that repeat over and over.

- ☞ The code body of a **Do-Loop While** loop always executes at least once, whereas you use a **Do While-Loop** when the body of the loop may or may not execute, depending on the relational test.

- ☞ Use **And** and **Or** to combine relational tests for more powerful loop testing.

- ☞ Stay away from infinite loops. Make sure the body of a loop changes the relational test that controls the loop.

**This page isn't blank—
it just looks that way.**

Chapter 22

Loop For as Long as You Need

In This Chapter

- Use **For** to control loops
- **For** loops count up and down as they execute
- You can nest one loop inside another

For is a Visual Basic statement that performs loops. Just as the **Do** loops repeat sections of code, so do **For** loops. You might wonder why yet another loop is necessary. With **For** and the two **Do** loops introduced in the previous chapter, you have three ways to loop through sections of code. (There are actually another two less-common **Do** loops as well, making a total of five ways to loop in Visual Basic!)

Just as there are several words in any spoken language that mean the same thing (*synonyms*, in grammar lingo), there is usually more than one way in any programming language to accomplish a job. The **For** loop repeats sections of code differently from **Do**, but you really don't *have* to have more than one way to loop; the choice of loop constructs is up to you.

A *construct* is a statement, such as **Do** or **For**, that controls a program.

Studying For

The format of **For** looks a little **For**eboding; so did the format of **Select Case**. However, and as you know, **Select Case** is fairly easy to understand. Here is the format of **For**:

> **For** *counterVar = start* **To** *end* [**Step** *increment*]
> *One or more Visual Basic statements*
> **Next** *counterVar*

Whereas the **Do** loops keep repeating while a certain relation is true, **For** loops loop for a specific number of times without resorting to a relational test.

As with all statement formats, the **Step** *increment* part of **For** is optional, and you don't always need it.

The **For** statement controls execution of a loop. During the execution, the *counterVar*, *start*, *end*, and *increment* statements control exactly how many times the loop loops.

We could walk through the **For** statement's format, but first a couple of examples should make things clearer.

The following code computes the sum of all the numbers from 1 to 5:

```
Total = 0
For num = 1 To 5
  Total = Total + num
Next num
```

num is the *counterVar* part of the **For** loop. **1** is the *start* part, and **5** is the *end* part. As you can see, the last two parts of **For** don't have to be variables, although *counterVar* always is a variable. Here is what you're telling Visual Basic:

*"Count up, from 1 to 5, storing each count in the variable named **num**. As you count, add the count to the value in **Total**."*

The *start* value is the first value assigned to the *counterVar* variable before the loop begins. Through the body of the loop, the *counterVar* variable, in this case **num**, contains the **1**. Then the **For** statement automatically updates the *counterVar* variable by adding 1 to it, and so **num** contains **2** through the second loop's iteration.

When *n* is added to a variable, the variable is said to be *incremented*. When *n* is subtracted, the variable is being *decremented*.

Perhaps this will help clarify this **For** loop. The following code does *exactly* the same thing, although it's not as elegant or compact, as the previous **For-Next** loop:

```
Total = 0
Total = Total + 1
Total = Total + 2
Total = Total + 3
Total = Total + 4
Total = Total + 5
```

When the loop executes only five times, the use of **For** may not be necessary. However, when the loop executes several hundred or a thousand times, isn't it easier to write three statements instead of several hundred or a thousand? Such large loops are not uncommon when your program must process every customer of a company or total each inventory item for tax purposes.

TECHNO NERD TEACHES...

The **Do** loops are great for the user's input validation, as shown in the last chapter. However, when a loop executes a fixed number of times, the **For** loop is a much better construct to use. The **For** loop automatically initializes and updates the loop's control variables for you and ends the loop whenever the *counterVar* variable becomes larger than the *end* variable.

continues

continued

Here is a **Do** loop that does the same thing as the previous **For**:

```
Total = 0
Count = 1
Do While (Count <= 5)
  Total = Total + Count
  Count = Count + 1
Loop
```

See, the updating of the loop control variable, **Count** in this case, is your full responsibility, as is the testing of when the loop should end.

A Different Step

For loops do not have to increment by 1. If you elect to add the **Step** option, you can specify a different increment and even a decrement if you prefer. The **Step** value changes the way that **For** updates the *counterVar* variable. If you don't specify **Step**, the **For** always assumes you want to step by 1. The following two **For** loop beginnings are exactly the same:

```
For i = 1 To 10
```

and

```
For i = 1 To 10 Step 1
```

If you want to increment the *counterVar* variable by 1, obviously it's easier to omit the **Step** portion of the **For** loop.

The following **For** loop counts by fives, because of the **Step 5** portion of the **For**:

```
Total = 0
For num = 5 To 25 Step 5
  Total = Total + num
Next num
```

When this loop finishes, **Total** will hold **75**, which is the total of **5, 10, 15, 20,** and **25**.

A **For** loop can count *down* as well. You can specify a negative **Step** value to count down. In other words, the following **For** loop does exactly the same thing as the previous loop, except the *counterVar* variable begins at **25** and counts down, by fives, to **5**:

```
Total = 0
For num = 25 To 5 Step -5
   Total = Total + num
Next num
```

When the **Step** value is negative, it's up to you to ensure that the *start* value is greater than the *end* value to ensure that a true countdown occurs.

The following example nicely demonstrates a negative **Step** value. Using the concatenation operator and the **Chr( )** function, the following **For** loop builds a **String** variable named **BackAlpha** that contains a reverse of the alphabet, from **Z** to **A**. See if you can figure out what's going on before reading the description.

```
Dim BackAlpha As String
Dim Char As Integer
For Char = 90 To 65 Step -1
   BackAlpha = BackAlpha + Chr(Char)
Next Char
MsgBox "Here is the string: " + BackAlpha
```

If you were to look at the ASCII table, you'd see that ASCII value **90** is the letter **Z**. As this **For** loop counts backward from 90 to 65, decrementing by **1**, the ASCII character for each numeric value is concatenated to the BackAlpha **String** variable. The loop stops after the **A**, ASCII value **65**, is concatenated. The MsgBox statement then displays the variable, as shown in Figure 22.1.

A **For** loop might never execute if the control variables' conditions don't work out. For example, the following **For** statement's body will never execute:

For i = 10 To 1 Step 5

Figure 22.1

*After building a string
from a backwards alphabet.*

Project1
Here is the string: ZYXWVUTSRQPONMLKJIHGFEDCBA
OK

A Glimpse of Really Hard Loops

A loop can appear within another loop. When that happens, the inner loop executes in full all of its iterations *each* time the outer loop iterates (Oh boy!). Consider the following code:

```
For Outer = 1 To 4
  For Inner = 1 To 3
    Beep
  Next Inner
Next Outer
```

A *nested* loop is one loop inside another loop. Nested loops don't belong just to the **For** statement. You also can nest **Do** loops.

The **Beep** statement simply buzzes the PC's speaker. How many times does this code beep the PC's speaker? The answer is neither 4 nor 3, but *12*. Picture the code without the inner loop. The **Beep** statement would execute only 4 times. However, the inner loop, which executes in full for each of the outer loop's 4 iterations, iterates *3* times. Therefore, you have a 3-time loop that executes 4 times!

This is often confusing to beginners. Surprisingly, unlike programs in other programming languages, Visual Basic programs don't often need nested loops because of the programs' event-driven style of code.

The Least You Need to Know

The **For** loop offers more control over your looping. When you have to repeat a section of code a fixed number of times, or use a loop to count up or down, a **For** loop works much better than a **Do** loop. The **For** takes care of behind-the-scenes details for you that the **Do** loops just don't handle. By changing the **Step** value, you control how much the **For** loop counts up or down through each loop's iteration. To use the **For** loop, you must know these things:

- ☞ **For** requires three values: A *counterVar* variable, a *start* value, and an *end* value. You will have to supply all three values to control your loops.

- ☞ Use **Step** if you want to increment by greater than 1 or by less than 1.

- ☞ You can nest loops by putting one inside the other. Both **For** and **Do** loops can be nested.

Blank (this) subliminal (book) message (is) page (great).

Chapter 23
Remarking on Advanced Code

In This Chapter

☛ Add remarks to improve your code's readability

☛ Use general subroutines to improve your code's structure

This chapter wraps up the last of the Visual Basic language discussion for this part of the book. You've about learned all the control statements that VB has to offer. (The important ones, anyway!) This chapter fills in some holes, teaches you how to describe, within the programs themselves, the programs you write, and prepares you with the background needed to start putting together larger VB programs than the ones you've seen so far.

Remarkable Remarks

You must write every program as if you will have to *re*write that program later. The world changes; you'll have to modify and update your programs to meet changing conditions. Despite the fact that programming is new to you now, it won't be long before you consider yourself an old pro at this game. You'll be writing hundreds of programs. Some of those will require additional work later, long after you thought you were done with them.

As a Visual Basic programmer, you understand the language. You now know several VB statements and you can probably look at simple programs and figure out their purpose. Many programs are extremely long, much longer than the ones you've seen so far. When you try to figure out a long program, with many hundreds of subroutines, it's easy to get bogged down in the code.

A remark is not a Visual Basic command. Remarks are descriptive lines that you put throughout your programs. The remarks are for *people*, not for Visual Basic. Visual Basic will ignore any and all remarks. Programmers put remarks throughout their code to describe what's happening.

Remarks help document your programs so you can understand them more easily later.

When you need to change a program, you can scan through the code to figure out what's happening—or you can read the remarks, if the programmer was thoughtful enough to provide them. It takes a lot less time to read remarks than to read code.

Adding Remarks

A remark always follows an apostrophe. When VB encounters an apostrophe, VB knows that the rest of the line is a remark for people, not more code that's needed to run the program. The following code comprises the first four lines in a longer routine. Of the four lines, three are remarks and one is a VB statement:

' Programmer: G. Will
'

' The following routine calculates salary
➥figures
Dim Salary As Single

You don't have to wade through the rest of the routine's VB code to figure out what the code is going to do. The code is a payroll calculation. Sure, the specifics are buried in the code, and you can look through them, but the third line, a remark, explains the purpose of the entire routine. When a VB application contains several functions, one or two lines of remarks dramatically improve your understanding of each routine.

The second line may not look like much, and it's not, but many programmers use empty remarks to separate lines of code and remarks from each other. Actually, VB is a *free-form* language, which means that you can add blank lines anywhere you wish without resorting to a remark, but programmers often use empty remarks anyway. The extra spacing is to make the program more readable. A book with short sentences and short paragraphs is easier to read than a Russian novel with page-long narrative paragraphs full of in-depth sentences. A program with lots of free-form empty space that makes the program more readable is also easier to read than a scrunched-up program.

It's common, especially in programming departments, for programmers to put their names at the top of the routines they write, as in the first line of this code. If a bug appears in the code later, or if the program needs to be changed, the original programmer can be contacted for blame or for help.

TECHNO NERD TEACHES...

Visual Basic still supports remarks that started back in the old days of the BASIC language. Any line that begins with **Rem** is considered a remark. The following two lines do exactly the same thing: They tell who wrote the program.

' Programmer: B. Dole

Rem Programmer: B. Dole

The apostrophe is used today more than **Rem**. Unlike **Rem**, the apostrophe can be used at the end of lines such as this:

Av = (Week1 + Week2 + Week3 + Week4) / 4   'Compute ➥ sales average

You cannot use **Rem** at the end of a line to explain the code.

Remarks Explain, Not Duplicate

Use remarks to describe a program, a routine, the programmer, and also code along the way. Scatter remarks throughout an entire subroutine if that subroutine needs explanation. Some code is easier to follow than other code. For example, the following line does not need a remark:

Total = 0

Placing a remark such as ' **Store 0 in Total** doesn't help explain that statement one bit. Use remarks with code that might be cryptic. Here is some code from the previous chapter, with remarks to help document what's going on. The remarks take the tedious *figuring out* out of the code if the programmer has to find the code and change it later:

```
' Store a backwards alphabet in a variable and display it
Dim BackAlpha As String      ' Will hold the letters
Dim Char As Integer           ' Used for the loop counter
For Char = 90 To 65 Step -1   ' Step back through ASCII values
   BackAlpha = BackAlpha + Chr(Char)   ' Append the next letter
Next Char
MsgBox "Here is the string: " + BackAlpha  ' Display the letters
```

Tying Together Some Things

As mentioned throughout this and other chapters, many programs consist of several routines. You've seen programs already that had several command buttons, each command button having a corresponding **Click()** subroutine. All the subroutines that you've written have depended on mouse clicks or the form loading or some other kind of event. You haven't yet seen two or more subroutines that depend on each other.

Programming is made up of all kinds of different routines. These routines, such as subroutines and functions, are not individual programs, but just pieces of one long program. Visual Basic inherently uses this building-block approach of using multiple routines.

SPEAK LIKE A GEEK

When one subroutine triggers the execution of another, the first subroutine is *calling* the second subroutine.

If you find yourself writing the same few lines in several subroutines, you might be better off turning those lines into their own named subroutine. When another routine needs those lines executed, you simply refer to the subroutine name, and VB executes that subroutine.

When one routine calls another, the calling code is placed on hold for a while. The called subroutine takes over, executes, and then control is returned to the calling code so that it can continue.

A subroutine is like a temporary detour that your code makes. Figure 23.1 shows you how the flow of execution occurs when one subroutine calls another.

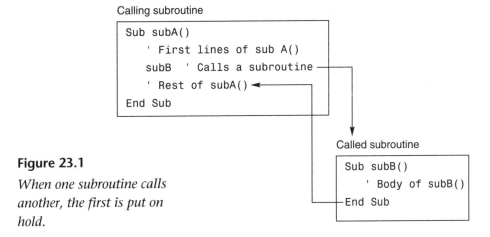

Figure 23.1

When one subroutine calls another, the first is put on hold.

A Subroutine Example

Remember that you cannot divide by zero? If you have a program that divides values, you must ensure that the user does not enter the value zero before dividing. In Chapter 19, "If True," you added division error checking to your CALC1.MAK program. The following subroutine occurred when the user clicked the / (divide) command button:

Notice that when you call a procedure, you don't put the parentheses after the name. (There are some advanced exceptions to this.)

```
Sub Command4_Click ()
    If (Val(txtNum2.Text) = 0) Then
```

```
      MsgBox "I can't divide by zero!", 0 + 48
   Else
      lblAnswer.Caption = Val(txtNum1.Text) / Val(txtNum2.Text)
   End If
   End Sub
```

The **MsgBox** error display lets the user know that division by zero cannot occur. The error is so serious that it would end the program like this:

```
   Sub Command4_Click ()
      If (Val(txtNum2.Text) = 0) Then
        Beep
        MsgBox "I can't divide by zero!", 0 + 48
        End
      Else
        lblAnswer.Caption = Val(txtNum1.Text) / Val(txtNum2.Text)
      End If
   End Sub
```

Beep gets the user's attention that a serious error occurred. The **End** makes the CALC1.MAK program very strict; if the user enters a zero, the program ends.

Suppose that the application contained several different kinds of calculators. There would be an easy four-function calculator, a scientific calculator, and a financial calculator. Each of the calculators would have a divide button, so all would need to check for a divide-by-zero error. All, therefore, would need these same three lines of code:

```
   Beep
   MsgBox "I can't divide by zero!", 0 + 48
   End
```

Although typing these three lines is relatively easy, you should consider putting the lines inside their own subroutine. (The subroutine's name might be **divideError()**.) There are two advantages to doing so:

☛ You don't have to type the three lines every place you need them. You only type them once, inside their subroutine. You'll save a little typing and decrease the chance of letting a typing error slip in.

☛ You make the program easier to maintain (update) later if needed, with the subroutine. The error code is in one location, not three. Therefore, if you change the way you handle the error, you only have to change the code in one place and not risk missing one of the sets of code.

Put It to Work

Load the CALC1.MAK application. With only a simple calculator, putting the error handler in its own subroutine might seem to be more trouble than it's worth. However, it would be good to learn about subroutines with this easy example.

The fourth command button, labeled /, is the command button that contains the divide code. Double-click the / command button and modify the **Command4_Click()** subroutine to look like this:

```
Sub Command4_Click ()
' Routine that divides if the second value is not zero
  If (Val(txtNum2.Text) = 0) Then
    Beep
    MsgBox "I can't divide by zero!", 0 + 48
    End    ' Stop the program after the serious error
  Else
    ' Update the Answer text box
    lblAnswer.Caption = Val(txtNum1.Text) / Val(txtNum2.Text)
  End If
End Sub
```

Instead of leaving the three lines where they are, let's create a new subroutine named **divideError()**. Until now, you opened the text editor for all new subroutines by double-clicking a control on the form. No control will trigger this new subroutine, though. Therefore, you have to be more specific about what kind of subroutine you're adding. You are now going to add a *general* subroutine as opposed to a subroutine tied to an object such as a form or command button.

Follow these steps to add the general subroutine:

If you're comfortable with Windows text editing, you could instead highlight the three lines in the **Command4_Click()** subroutine that forms the body of the new routine, save the lines to the Clipboard (with **Ctrl+C**), and insert the three lines in the **divideError()** window when you open it. Then, you'd only have to add the **Sub** and **End Sub** statements. (I know, this is a fine time to tell you that!)

If you ever want to jump between procedures quickly, press **F2** (or select Procedures from the Window menu), and VB displays the procedure selection dialog box you see in Figure 23.2.

1. With the **Command4_Click()** subroutine still on your screen, click the **down arrow** to the right of the **Object:** scroll box at the top of the code window. You see a list of objects for which you can write subroutines.

2. Scroll the list upward (by clicking the **up arrow**) until you see the word **(general)**. Click on **(general)**, and VB will open a blank code window for the new subroutine you're about to write.

3. Type the following. Be very careful to type the code just as you see it here:

```
Sub divideError ()
  Beep
  MsgBox "I can't divide by zero!", 0 + 48
  End    ' Stop the program after the serious
➥error
End Sub
```

4. You've just added a new general subroutine. As with all subroutines, **divideError()** has beginning and ending **Sub** and **End Sub** statements. You must now return to the **Command4_Click()** subroutine and eliminate the code that you've put in the new general subroutine.

   Click on the **Object:** scroll list again and select **Command4**.

5. Delete the three lines from the **Beep** to the **End** that you put in the **divideError()** routine. In their place, add this single line:

   divideError   ' Call the error handler

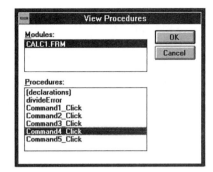

Figure 23.2

You can easily move from one procedure to another.

6. You're ready to try out your creation! Press **F5** and click / before entering a value for the second number. You'll hear a beep, see a message box appear, and the program will end when you press **Enter** at the message box. Your subroutine takes over! Save the project and take a break.

Give your subroutines names that describe their actions. Then, when you display a list of subroutines, you'll be able to tell what each one in the list does because of its name.

The Least You Need to Know

Remarks help document your programs so you can modify the programs later without wading through a lot of code. The remarks also describe who wrote the program so the original programmer can be found if problems arise (this may be needed in companies with large programming staffs). Add remarks *as* you write the program for the first time— programmers *rarely* add them later!

Once you've improved your coding with remarks, break long subroutines, or common code, into separate subroutines. It's a lot better to consolidate code that appears throughout your application into separate subroutines so it's easier to modify later and your program is easier to follow. Remember the following if you want maintainable programs:

☛ Remarks help document your program. Use remarks abundantly in your VB programs.

continues

continued

- ☞ As a shortcut, use an apostrophe, ', to begin remarks.

- ☞ Separate common code into stand-alone general subroutines to facilitate your programming tasks.

- ☞ Press **F2** to select another subroutine to edit.

Part V
Get Exotic: More Neat Controls

If the only controls that Visual Basic had to offer were command buttons, labels, and text boxes, you'd still create great programs such as the ones you've been seeing so far.

Visual Basic always goes an additional step to beat the competition. Actually, Visual Basic has tons *of controls that are really neat and easy to use and that snap up your applications. You've seen the toolbox, so you already know that there are many controls you can tap into.*

The type of control you select for an application depends on what that application needs to do at the time. The next few chapters explore a few more controls and show you how to access the potential of the controls. Virtually everything you already know about controls, such as properties and placement on the form, applies to the rest of the controls. Therefore, you'll find that the new controls are simple to use.

Sometimes, it's almost too easy to add fancy controls to Visual Basic programs. That's the fun of Visual Basic: Try a control, and if it doesn't fit into your program the way you originally expected that it would, replace the control with another that might suit the job better.

Chapter 24
Option Buttons

In This Chapter

- ☛ Option buttons give users choices
- ☛ Only one option button is selected at any one time
- ☛ Option Button controls are easy to understand

If you've used a Windows program before, you've no doubt seen option buttons. Option buttons give you a multiple-choice selection of options. The important thing to remember is that you can only select *one* of the options at any one time.

Take a moment to study Figure 24.1. The program has three option buttons toward the right of the screen. After typing a value in US currency, the user clicks an option button to see a foreign currency equivalent value. The user can select only one foreign currency at a time (the Option Button controls ensure this). In this chapter you'll build the application shown in Figure 24.1.

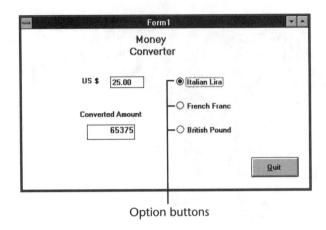

Figure 24.1

Three option buttons give you a choice.

Option buttons

Preparing for the Option Buttons

Before getting to the option buttons, go ahead and create the window with everything *except* the three Option Button controls. Figure 24.2 contains the Form window without the option buttons to give you an idea of where to place and how to size the controls.

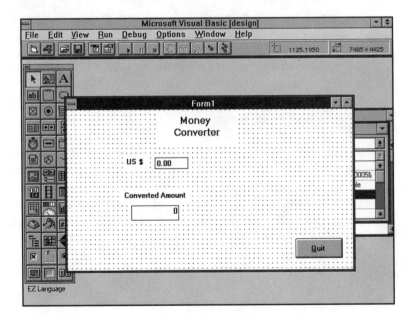

Figure 24.2

Getting ready for the option buttons.

In creating an application that matches the one in Figure 24.1, keep in mind the following points about the application's non-Option Button controls:

- ☛ The top label, the title of the screen, has an Alignment of **2—Center** and a FontSize of **12**. If you'd like a more appealing title, select a fancy Windows True Type FontName property for the label.

- ☛ **US $** is a label, resized to hold the caption.

- ☛ The first Text Box control, to the right of **US $**, has an Alignment property of **0—Left Justify**, a BorderStyle property of **1—Fixed Single**, the Name **USAmt**, and a Text property of **0.00**.

- ☛ The number beneath the **Converted Amount** label is also a Label control. Change the control's Alignment property to **1—Right Justify**. Change the BorderStyle to **1—Fixed Single**, the Caption to **0**, the FontSize to **9.75**, and the Name to **ConvAmt**.

- ☛ The command button contains the Caption property **&Quit**.

Adding the Option Buttons

You must add the Option Button controls one at a time. (Visual Basic cannot read your mind and know that you want three option buttons! Some programs are *so* limited!) Add them just as you add any other control: Either double-click the option button (the button on the toolbox with a circle containing a black dot) or, better yet, now that you've got other controls on the form, click the Option Button control and move the mouse cursor to the form, then anchor and size the option button right where you want it.

Add the first Option Button control. Type **Italian Lira** for the Caption property and resize the option button so that the caption fits. Set the Value property to **True**. As soon as you do so, Visual Basic selects the option button by darkening its circle. Now set it back to **False**, because for now you want none of

As with **If** relational tests, an Option Button control can have only one of two values: **True** or **False**. The Option Button control is either clicked (**True**) or it's not (**False**).

Only one Option Button control on a form can be **True** at any one time. (Oh, there's an advanced exception to this, but don't worry about it now.)

the three option buttons to be selected when the program starts. (I had you set it to **True** just to see what would happen.)

Add the second and third Option Button controls. Specify **French Franc** for the second Caption property and **British Pound** for the third Option Button control's Caption property.

Adding the Code

The only thing left to do is add code to tie all this together. Start with the easy code. Double-click the command button and type **End** for the body of the **Quit** button so the user has a way to quit the program.

Now that that's out of the way, close the code window (**Alt+F4**) and double-click the first option button (the one labeled **Italian Lira**). Visual Basic opens the **Option1_Click()** subroutine. Add code to the subroutine's body so the subroutine ends up looking like this:

```
Sub Option1_Click ()
' Convert the US amount to Italian Lira
    ConvAmt.Caption = 2615 * USAmt.Text
End Sub
```

Have you noticed yet that Visual Basic turns your remarks green? That's just an added bonus. You can glance through a code window looking for remarks or code, and the color difference helps you find what you want.

You don't have to return to the Form window just to choose another code window. Click the **Object:** pull-down window and select **Option2**. Visual Basic opens a new **Option2_Click()** code window so that you can add this code:

```
Sub Option2_Click ()
' Convert the US amount to French Francs
    ConvAmt.Caption = 11.8 * USAmt.Text
End Sub
```

You can figure out what's next. Click the **Option:** pull-down list, select **Option3**, and make sure the following ends up in the code window:

```
Sub Option3_Click ()
' Convert the US amount to British Pounds
   ConvAmt.Caption = .75 * USAmt.Text
End Sub
```

Run the program to give the Option Button controls a spin! Change the **0.00** in the **US $** text box to another value and click the three Option Button controls in any order. The **Converted Amount** label changes to reflect the converted value.

When options are *mutually exclusive*, as they are with Option Button controls, only one can be selected at any one time.

Option buttons are often called *radio buttons*. Before digital electronics became so popular, car radios had a series of five or six buttons. Pressing a button chose a station. (You remember, don't you?) When you pressed a button, that button stayed in until you pressed *another* button. Only one could be selected at any one time, just as only one option button can be selected at any one time.

The Least You Need to Know

This chapter was short! Actually, the brevity of the chapter is attributable to the base of knowledge you had when you began the chapter. With what you already know, this material is very easy indeed. In this chapter, you learned about Option Button controls. Option buttons are needed when you want to provide a mutually exclusive set of options from which the user can choose. You should take from this chapter the following:

- ☞ Option buttons provide for a mutually exclusive set of choices.

- ☞ Option buttons can be set only to **True** or **False**.

- ☞ Only one option button in a group can be selected at any one time. That button's value is **True**, while all the others (which are not selected) have a **False** value.

No, this is not a printing error.
The page truly is blank.

Chapter 25
Check Your Check Boxes

In This Chapter

- ☞ You can provide users with Check Box controls

- ☞ More than one check box can be set at a time

- ☞ The **Format()** function makes your output look exactly the way you want it to look

Option buttons are great for giving users multiple choices, but as you saw in the previous chapter, the user can select only *one* option button at a time. What if you need to let the user choose zero or more of the options? You use *Check Box controls* for giving the user several options to select.

You've seen check boxes in Windows applications. When you click one or more of the check boxes with the mouse, an **X** appears in the check box, turning on that option. Check boxes (like option buttons) might be listed in a row across the window or up and down the window. Figure 25.1 shows a modified currency conversion program with two Check Box controls at the bottom of the screen.

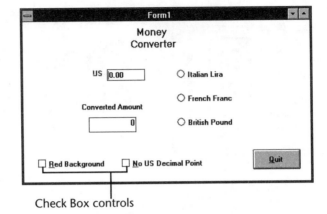

Figure 25.1

Adding check boxes to an application.

Check Box controls

It's easy to know when to use check boxes and when to use option buttons. The check boxes are needed for the two bottom controls because it's possible that the user wants a red background *and* no decimal points displayed. Option buttons had to be used for the three European currencies, though, because only one can be selected at any one time.

Change the Currency Application a Bit

You may have noticed that the text box to the right of Figure 25.1's **US $** label is slightly longer than the one in Chapter 24. Load the currency application and extend the length of the **USAmt** text box so that its Width property is **855**, to match the one in Figure 25.1. This accuracy isn't really needed at this point, but it will ensure that your screen matches this chapter's figures as closely as possible.

One nice thing about Visual Basic is that, because you can click and drag the mouse, it's easy to change widths, lengths, and placements of controls. You can run a program, look at the screen, and easily adjust elements on the screen by returning to the Form window to make those adjustments. If you find that you haven't given enough room to a text box or label, it's easy to adjust it.

Although today's C and C++ compilers are *finally* catching up to Visual Basic's screen element placement ability, it used to take tedious text editing of a *resource script* (whatever *that* is) to make a minor adjustment to a control's size. Visual Basic has given its users this visual ease of adjustment ever since Visual Basic's Version 1.0 hit the market.

Time for the Check Boxes

Add the check boxes that you see at the bottom of Figure 25.1. The Check Box control appears on the toolbox as a square with an X in the center of the square (the third control from the top in the first row for Professional Edition owners and the fourth control from the top in the first row for Standard Edition owners).

Place the first check box at the window's bottom left. This is the check box that's about to become the **Red Background** check box. Change the Caption property to **&Red Background**.

Although your check box doesn't have to match Figure 25.1's exactly, here are the size and placement property values of the figure's check box in case you want to match them:

Height: **375**
Left: **360**
Top: **3360**
Width: **1815**

Add the second check box to the right of the first one. Here are the second check box's vital property values:

Caption: **&No US Decimal Point**
Height: **375**
Left: **2520**
Top: **3360**
Width: **2175**

The **&** before the **R** in **Red** ensures that you'll have an access key, **Alt+R**, to the check box. It's common to add access key support to check boxes so users can check the box either with a keystroke or with the mouse.

Time for the Code

Are you getting the idea by now that adding new and exciting controls isn't any harder than adding labels, command buttons, and text boxes? It's true. Rest assured, you think this is easy because it is. If everybody knew how easy Visual Basic is, the whole industry would switch to it. (Let's keep this between us...)

After adding the code behind the check boxes, you'll be through with this application. In adding the code, however, you're going to learn about a neat way to format numeric values so they look the way you want. There'll be more about that in a couple sections.

The Red Background

Why would the user want the background to be red? Maybe she or he wouldn't, but adding this feature provides a simple introduction to Check Box controls.

Some very powerful Windows programs have only a single Form window as their backgrounds.

There is only one form in this application, as has been the case with all other applications in this book. The form name is **Form1**. You can change the form name if you like, through the form's Properties window, but **Form1** is fine for this application.

Add functionality to the first check box by following these steps:

1. Double-click the first check box control to open its **Check1_Click()** code window.

2. Add the following text to the body of the subroutine:

```
If Check1.Value = 1 Then
  Form1.BackColor = QBColor(4)
Else
  Form1.BackColor = QBColor(15)
End If
```

When a check box is clicked (when its **X** appears), the Value property of that check box is **1**. When a check box is left unclicked by the user, the Value property is **0**. This code executes when and only when the user clicks the check box to turn the **X** display on or off. When clicked, the **If** statement looks at the Value property. If a **1** is found, the form's background changes to red (the **QBColor()** value for red is **4**, as you learned in Chapter 10, "Change Properties Through Code"). Otherwise (**Else**) the value is changed or left at **15**, which is the **QBColor()** value for white.

3. Close the code window and double-click the second check box to open its code window. Add the following code to the body of **Check2_Click()**:

   If Check2.Value = 1 Then
     USAmt.Text = Format(USAmt.Text, "######")
   Else
     USAmt.Text = Format(USAmt.Text, "#####.00")
   End If

4. Press **F5** to run the program. Enter **200.00** for the US currency amount. Click the **Italian Lira** option button. Now click the **Red Background** check box to make the form's background red. Click the check box again, and the red goes away because the check box is no longer clicked.

What's that **Format** stuff in the code? You'll learn about it in the next section.

5. Click the **No US Decimal Point** check box to see the decimal point and two decimal places go away to the right of **US $**. Click the check box again, and the decimals reappear.

6. Click both the **Red Background** and the **No US Decimal Point** check boxes. Unlike with option buttons, there is nothing wrong with checking both of the boxes. Your screen will look something like the one in Figure 25.2.

You don't have to click right over the square next to **Red Background**. You can click anywhere over the words **Red Background** or press **Alt+R** to turn the check box on and off.

7. Close the application with the **Quit** command button.

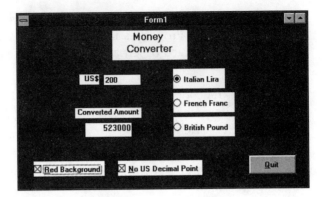

Figure 25.2

Checking both check boxes is possible.

The Format() Function

Visual Basic does its best to display numeric values in the way it thinks is best. What is best for one application, however, isn't always best for another. When displaying dollar amounts, sometimes you want two decimal places for the cents and sometimes you want whole dollar amounts. What you almost *never* want, however, is a single decimal place or three decimal places, such as **$5.2** or **$5.295**, because the values don't match commonly used dollar and cent amounts.

The reason that the currency application displays two decimal places, **0.00**, next to **US $** when you first start the program is simply because the text box's Text property contains **0.00**. The user is free to enter some value that does *not* have two decimal places, but as soon as the user clicks the second check box, the code behind the form takes control and formats the user's **US $** value either to two decimal places or to none at all.

Format() is a built-in function that formats numeric values to look the way you want them to look. Here is how the **Format()** function is often used:

variable = Format(*variable*, *formatString*)

If the same *variable* appears on the left of the equals sign and also as **Format()**'s first argument, you are changing the format of a numeric variable. If a different *variable* appears to the left of the equals sign, you aren't changing a *variable*'s format but storing a newly formatted variable in another variable.

Always keep in mind that **Format()** returns a **Variant** data type. As long as you format a numeric variable, its formatted value is **Variant** (as are all control values by default) so you can later compute from the formatted value.

The *formatString* must be a string constant enclosed inside quotation marks. There are fixed *formatString*s and programmer-defined *formatString*s. Table 25.1 lists some of the fixed *formatString*s.

Table 25.1   Common Values for Fixed *formatStrings*

Common *formatString* Value	Description
"Currency"	Displays a dollar sign before the value, a *thousands separator* (a decimal point or comma, depending on the country your computer is set for), and two decimal places. Also, negative values are enclosed in parentheses.
"Fixed"	Displays at least one digit before and two to the right of the decimal point, with no thousands separator.
"Percent"	Multiplies the number by 100 and adds a percent sign, %, to the value.
"Yes/No"	Displays **Yes** if the value contains anything besides zero and displays **No** if the value contains a **0**.
"True/False"	Displays **True** if the value contains anything but zero and displays **False** if the value contains a **0**.

There are more *formatString* values, but those listed in Table 25.1 are the most common ones.

Be sure that you enclose these **Format()** values in quotation marks. You might wonder why the **US $** amount was formatted with those funny-looking pound signs (#) instead of using "**Currency**" in the **Format()** function. With "**Currency**", there would then be *two* dollar signs appearing to the left of the **US $** value: one at the end of the **US** label and the other at the beginning of the value field.

Before working with the pound signs, take a moment to study the following **Format()** values. The remark before each **Format()** function call describes what's being assigned to the variable named **FValue**.

```
Dim FValue As Variant
' The next assignment stores $12,345.68 in FValue
FValue = Format(12345.678, "Currency")
' The next assignment stores 12345.68 in FValue
FValue = Format(12345.678, "Fixed")
' The next assignment stores 52.00% in FValue
FValue = Format(.52, "Percent")
' The next assignment stores Yes in FValue
FValue = Format(1, "Yes/No")
' The next assignment stores False in FValue
FValue = Format(0, "True/False")
```

Not all of the predefined formats match what you'll want, although most of them do. Each of the numeric formats supplies a decimal point, but the check box at the bottom of the currency application requests that no decimal point be displayed. Also, when the box is not checked, the user will want to see two decimal places and a thousands separator, but never a dollar sign before the number, because there is already a dollar sign there.

If you need to define your own numeric **Format()**, you can use a combination of pound signs and zeros to do what you want. There are many other format characters, but pound signs and zeros are the ones that you'll use most.

A pound sign indicates where a digit is to go. If you insert a decimal point inside a string of pound signs, you tell VB where to put the decimal point. (As always, the decimal point is actually a comma if you've set up your computer for many non-US countries.) Therefore, the following statement, which is inside the **Check2_Click()** function:

> **USAmt.Text = Format(USAmt.Text, "#####")**

tells VB to format whatever value is in the Text property of the **USAmt** text box with five places, no decimal point, and no fractional portion. VB rounds up if the value contains a fraction greater than or equal to **.5**.

Everywhere there is a **0** in a programmer-defined **Format()** string, VB ensures that some digit will appear, either a valid fractional digit or a zero if there is no digit to print. In other words, if you were to format the value **123.4** with the **"#####.00"** format string, VB would format the value as **123.40** (notice the two spaces for the missing digits to the left of the decimal point). A value such as **123.4567** would format as **123.46** to maintain the two decimal places at all times.

The statement

> **USAmt.Text = Format(USAmt.Text, "#####.00")**

simply instructs Visual Basic to format the value with two decimal places and always display the two decimal places even if the value is a whole dollar amount.

> ## The Least You Need to Know
>
> Check boxes let you provide independent choices for your user. A user might check none, one, or all check boxes on the screen. When the user checks a box, the box's Value property becomes **True**, and your code can look for that condition and act appropriately.
>
> You also learned how to format numeric values using the predefined format strings as well as how to define your own format strings. You'll no longer have to settle for money amounts that don't look like money amounts! In this chapter you learned the following:
>
> *continues*

continued

☞ The user can check one or more check boxes at a time, unlike option buttons.

☞ Check boxes are set to **True** or **False**, corresponding to **1** or **0**.

☞ The built-in **Format()** function lets you control the way your numeric output looks.

☞ You can use a predefined format string inside **Format()** or define your own format string.

Chapter 26

List Boxes
Offer Choices

In This Chapter

☛ List boxes offer another way to give your user choices

☛ The **AddItem** method puts items in the list box

☛ You can instruct Visual Basic to sort your list box items for you

A *List Box control* is a control that gives your users a choice. You've seen list boxes when you've chosen from the Visual Basic File Open dialog box. A list box is a box with a list of choices from which the user can select.

This chapter changes the currency application so that a list box appears instead of option boxes. With the list box, you save some screen real estate because not every option has to be displayed at the same time. In addition, list boxes are a good introduction to the Combo Box controls that you'll read about in the next chapter.

Get Rid of the Check Boxes

You've got to make room for a new list box in the currency application. Therefore, load the currency application if you no longer have it loaded from the previous chapter. You haven't had to remove controls from a form yet, so this section will show you how.

There are two ways to remove controls from a form:

☞ You can remove one control at a time.

☞ If the controls appear right next to each other or right on top of each other you can remove the entire group.

There are three option boxes in the currency program. You'll first remove a single control and then remove the last two at the same time. When you remove a control, you also remove all code behind that control. Therefore, the **Option1_Click()** code no longer exists after you remove the control. You'll have to add it later when you add the list box.

Put It to Work

Click on the top option box, labeled **Italian Lira**. When the resizing handles appear, you can remove the entire control by pressing the **Del** key. As soon as you press **Del**, Visual Basic removes the control.

If you ever want to move a group of controls that are near each other on a form, you can select them all and move them as a group instead of one at a time.

To remove the last two controls, you must draw a selection box around the controls you want to remove. Here's how:

1. Make sure the arrow on the toolbox is highlighted.

2. Move the mouse cursor to a position right above and to the left of the remaining option boxes (above and to the left of the option box labeled **French Franc**).

3. Click and hold the mouse button while dragging the lower-right corner of the selection box until both option boxes are enclosed in the selection box, as shown in Figure 26.1. As the figure shows, the dotted selection box goes away as soon as you release the mouse button, but you know the two option boxes are enclosed in the selection because their resizing handles show.

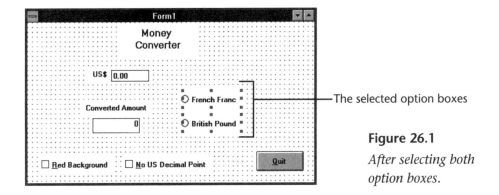

The selected option boxes

Figure 26.1

After selecting both option boxes.

4. With the two option buttons selected, press **Del**, and both disappear. You've now removed the option boxes and you can replace them with a list box.

A list box is not inherently better than option boxes. However, a list box does allow for a longer list of values. As you'll see later in this chapter, if a list box contains several items, Visual Basic will provide a scroll bar so the user can scroll through the options in the list box.

Adding the List Box

Figure 26.2 shows the List Box control on the toolbox. If you have the Standard Edition of Visual Basic, the List Box control is the fourth tool of the toolbox's second column.

The List Box control ——

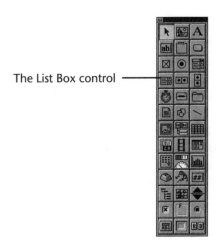

Figure 26.2

Finding the List Box control.

Place a list box approximately where the option boxes were. Set the following properties for the list box so that your program matches the one in this chapter as closely as possible.

Height: **615**
Left: **3960**
Sorted: **True**
Top: **1680**
Width: **1935**

The most interesting property you set is the Sorted property. Visual Basic will now automatically alphabetically sort any data that appears in the list box.

The three foreign currency names have to appear in the list box, but there are no properties that let you add items such as list box items. You must use a built-in routine called **AddItem**.

AddItem is not a subroutine or a function. **AddItem** is called a *method*. You execute a method using a *dot operator*.

Filling the List Box

Before the user sees the form, you must, with code, put items in the list box. Anytime that you need to initialize list boxes, variables, or any other element of a VB program, perhaps the best place to initialize those elements is in the **Form_Load()** function. **Form_Load()** is a function that Visual Basic executes right before the user sees the form on the screen.

To open the **Form_Load()** function, double-click the mouse pointer anywhere on the form. Visual Basic opens the **Form_Load()** text-editing window and prepares the opening and closing statements of the function. Fill in the body of the **Form_Load()** function so that it looks like this:

```
Sub Form_Load ()
    List1.AddItem "Italian Lira"
```

List1.AddItem "French Franc"
List1.AddItem "British Pound"
End Sub

You're smart and you can easily see what's going on. You must add the **AddItem** method to the end of the list box name, **List1**. **AddItem** adds items—the string items to the right of **AddItem**—to the list box. If you want to add items to a specific list location (and this is rare), you can append a number at the end of the **AddItem** line. **0** adds an item to the beginning of the list. For example, if you were to insert the following line right before the previous code's **End Sub** (don't add this yet):

You still need to add code to compute the currency conversions! Running the program at this time simply gives you an idea of what the program's output will look like.

List1.AddItem "German Mark " 0

then **German Mark** would appear before **Italian Lira** in the resulting list box. Don't add **German Mark** at this time, however.

You rarely need to specify the location of items in a list box because the Sorted property keeps the items sorted no matter in which order you added the items.

After adding the **Form_Load()** code shown previously, press **F5** to run the program. You'll see the screen shown in Figure 26.3. Click any item in the list box, use the arrow keys to highlight the other items, and then press the **Quit** command button.

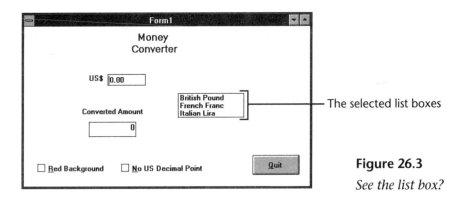

— The selected list boxes

Figure 26.3
See the list box?

Adding Code Behind the List

Visual Basic provides an interesting way for your program to know when the user clicks an item in the list box. When the user clicks an item anywhere in the list box, VB executes the **List1_Click()** procedure. Of course, if you were to rename the list box something other than **List1**, the name of the function would change also.

When the Form window reappears, open the **List1_Click()** code window by double-clicking the list box. The Text property of the list box changes, depending on what the user highlights when the program executes. Therefore, most code processing of list boxes is little more than a big **Select Case** that checks the Text property of the list box inside **List1_Click()**. Edit the **List1_Click()** code so that it reads as follows:

```
Sub List1_Click ()
  Select Case List1.Text
    Case "Italian Lira":
      ' Convert the US amount to Italian Lira
      ConvAmt.Caption = 2615 * USAmt.Text
    Case "French Franc":
      ' Convert the US amount to French Francs
      ConvAmt.Caption = 11.8 * USAmt.Text
    Case "British Pound":
      ' Convert the US amount to British Pounds
      ConvAmt.Caption = .75 * USAmt.Text
  End Select
End Sub
```

See that the list box items are alphabetized? Visual Basic alphabetized the list because earlier you changed the Sorted property to **True**.

You'll recognize that the calculations are the same as those used for the individual check boxes that you saw when you first created this application. Run the program and enter a US dollar amount. Click the various list box items and watch the converted amount change accordingly. Click **Quit** to terminate the program.

An Added Bonus

Visual Basic doesn't care if you add more items to a list box than will fit at one time. The size of this application's list box is only enough to show three items. However, you can easily add more by adding additional items to the **Form_Load()** routine.

Double-click the **Form_Load()** routine and add the following two lines right before the **End Sub** statement:

```
List1.AddItem "German Mark"
List1.AddItem "Hong Kong Dollar"
```

You'll also have to update the **List1_Click()** code to handle the additional conversions. Open the **List1_Click()** subroutine and add these lines before the **End Select** statement:

```
Case "German Mark":
 ' Convert the US amount to German Marks
 ConvAmt.Caption = 4 * USAmt.Text
Case "Hong Kong Dollar":
 ' Convert the US amount to Hong Kong Dollars
 ConvAmt.Caption = USAmt.Text / .18
```

Run the program and you will see scroll bars on the list box. The scroll bars are the primary reason that List Box controls are preferred over separate option boxes. All the items in check boxes must appear on the screen, whereas the list box can be small and yet hold many values.

The Least You Need to Know

The List Box control is needed when you want to give your users lots of choices but you don't want a bunch of option boxes taking up lots of screen space. You must add items to the list box in a **Form_Load( )** routine, but **AddItem** makes adding items simple enough. Here's what you've learned in this chapter:

☞ List boxes offer users a list of options from which to choose. Your choice of option, check, or list boxes depends on your application's needs.

☞ The user can choose only one list box item at a time.

☞ Use the **AddItem** method to put items in the List Box control.

☞ Scroll bars automatically display when lots of items appear in a list box, so you don't have to worry about items taking too much list box space.

Chapter **27**

A Combo Is Jumbo!

In This Chapter

- ☛ Learn about the two combo boxes
- ☛ Use **AddItem** and **RemoveItem** for combo box entries
- ☛ Move the focus around the screen

There are two kinds of Combo Box controls, and they are similar to but not exactly like list boxes. You saw in the previous chapter that a list box provides, with optional scroll bars, options from which your user can choose. A combo box lets the user add or delete items in the list, whereas a list box lets the user highlight only items already in the list.

The two kinds of combo boxes are *drop-down combo boxes* and *simple combo boxes*. Figure 27.1 shows one of each.

There is a third kind of combo box, which is nothing more than a drop-down list box. This chapter covers only the two most common combo boxes, the ones shown in Figure 27.1.

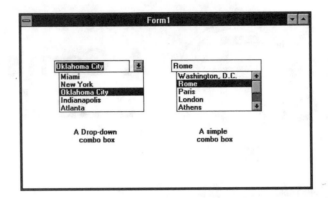

Figure 27.1

The two kinds of combo boxes.

If the Combo Box control's Sort property is set to **True**, Visual Basic always displays the combo box contents in alphabetical order. Gee, in other programming languages, you have to write a sorting routine to do that sort of thing!

Creating a Simple Combo Box Application

In this chapter, you'll create a simple application that uses combo boxes. First, we'll start with a drop-down combo box and then we'll convert the application to a simple combo box.

The application will simply be a famous-person tracker. That is, the user will enter names of famous people she or he has met. (It's corny, but it'll do nicely!) Figure 27.2 shows the program's window after the user enters several people's names.

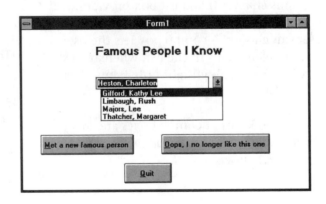

Figure 27.2

A famous person list-keeping program.

Begin by adding the title label and the three command buttons. Follow these steps:

1. Add the title label and enter **Famous People I Know** for the caption. Here are the properties of the label that you'll need for this application:

   Alignment: **2—Center**
   FontSize: **13.5**
   Height: **495**
   Left: **1800**
   Top: **360**
   Width: **3495**

2. Add the **Met a new famous person** command button. Here are the button's properties:

   Caption: **&Met a new famous person**
   Height: **495**
   Left: **480**
   Name: **Met**
   Top: **2640**
   Width: **2415**

3. Add the **Oops, I no longer like this one** command button. Here are the button's properties:

   Caption: **&Oops, I no longer like this one**
   Height: **495**
   Left: **3600**
   Name: **Oops**
   Top: **2640**
   Width: **2775**

4. Add the **Quit** command button. It's easy, and the only thing you have to do is make sure its Caption property reads **&Quit**.

5. Double-click the **Quit** command button, and insert the **End** statement into the subroutine's body. Close the code window.

The left command button will add items to the combo box and the right command button will remove items from the combo box.

Time for the Combo Box

Now you've got to add the combo box. Figure 27.3 shows where the Combo Box control is on the toolbox. (If you have the Standard Edition, the Combo Box control appears as the fifth control from the top in the toolbox's first column.)

—The Combo Box control

Figure 27.3

The Combo Box control's location.

Double-click the Combo Box control. Perhaps it's easiest to go straight to the Properties window (**F4**) and enter these non-default values:

Height: **300** (You can't change it if you try! It's read-only.)
Left: **1920**
Sorted: **True**
Style: **0—Dropdown Combo** (the default)
Text: (Leave blank)
Top: **1200**
Width: **3255**

A *read-only* property is a property that is fixed and that you cannot change.

If you were to run the program (you can now, but it won't work correctly yet), you could type people's names into the combo box, but the command button to add the name is not yet hooked up, with code, to the combo box. The combo box does not automatically add items to its list. As you may have guessed, as with the List Box control, you must use the **AddItem** method to add items to a combo box.

When the user wants to add an item to the combo box, the user will have to do two things:

1. Type the name in the combo box.

2. Click the left-hand command button to add the name.

Connecting with Code

Double-click the left-hand command button. You named this command button **Met**, so the subroutine that VB opens is called **Met_Click()**. Add the following code to the body of **Met_Click()**:

If the user (*you*, in this case!) were to type a name into the combo box but fail to click the left-hand command button, the name would not go to the list.

```
Dim FamousPerson As String
FamousPerson = Combo1.Text
Combo1.AddItem FamousPerson  ' Add name to combo list
Combo1.Text = ""   ' Null string in combo's text box
```

Creating the **String** variable named **FamousPerson** wasn't really necessary, but it does store the value typed by the user in case you later want to expand this application further (for example, by adding disk access to hold the names after the user exits the application).

The user's input in the combo box always goes into the combo box's Text property. Therefore, the second line of this code saves the user's input in the **FamousPerson** variable. The third line then adds that name to the combo box. **AddItem** takes the user's input at the top of a combo box and adds that full input to the combo box list of items. Visual Basic inserts the item alphabetically into the combo box list because of the True Sorted property.

Keep in mind that this code belongs to the left-hand command button, not to the combo box. This code executes only after the user types a name at the top of the combo box and then clicks the left-hand command button.

The fourth line clears the user's input from the top of the combo box to prepare the application for a new name.

Close the code window and double-click the right-hand command button. Removing combo box items requires the **RemoveItem** method. Add the following code to the **Oops_Click()** command button's subroutine body:

```
' Remove the highlighted item, indexed with
' ListIndex, if the user has highlighted someone
If Combo1.ListIndex >= 0 Then
    Combo1.RemoveItem Combo1.ListIndex
Else
    ' Don't do anything
End If
```

Each of the items in a combo box is indexed with a number from 0 to one less than the number of items in the list. The first combo box name will have a ListIndex value of **0**, the second **1**, and so on. (This is the same index you can add to the end of the **AddItem** method to insert items at specific locations in a list box as described in the previous chapter.)

The **If** simply ensures that the current value of the ListIndex property is equal to or more than **0**. If the user had not highlighted a name before clicking this command button, the ListIndex property would not pass the **If** test, and nothing would happen (no name can be deleted). If a name is selected, **RemoveItem** erases the name and updates the combo box.

Running the Application

For your first combo box application, it will help to walk through a run of the program. You'll see that an extra step is needed, when adding the names, which might now seem unnecessary. Run the program (**F5**) and follow these steps:

1. Type **Lassie** in the combo box.

2. Press **Alt+M** or click the left-hand command button to add the name to the combo box.

   Lassie goes away from the combo box. Actually, **Lassie** is a part of the combo box's list of names, but the name won't appear in the data-entry portion of the combo box. You'll display the contents of the combo box in a moment.

3. Press **Shift+Tab** or again click the combo box's data-entry section to enter another name. (This is the step that might seem redundant, and we'll automate it later.)

4. Enter **Benji** in the combo box, and again press **Alt+M** to add the name.

5. Press **Shift+Tab** or click the mouse to return to the combo box's entry section. Now click the **down arrow** to the right of the list box. You can see the contents of the box now!

6. Add one more name, **Rover**, to the combo box. Don't forget to press **Alt+M**.

Now remove a name. When removing items from a combo box, Visual Basic erases the name from the list and closes the gap where the name was. You must remove a name using these two steps:

1. Highlight the name you want to remove.

2. Click the right-hand command button to remove the item (thus triggering the **Oops_Click()** subroutine).

After you remove a name, display the combo box again (click on its **down arrow** or highlight the combo box and press **Alt+down arrow**), and you'll see that Visual Basic removed the name.

Focus Better

A simple addition that will greatly improve the program is finding some way to move the focus (the control that's active) back to the combo box after adding or removing a name. It's no fun doing the two-step when you want to add or remove several names in the list.

The **SetFocus** method moves the focus to whatever control you specify. **SetFocus** is a method versus a built-in function, so you know that you must use the dot operator to set the focus. Here is the general format of **SetFocus**:

ControlName.SetFocus

Anywhere in your application's code, at any time, when you want to move the focus to a specific control, call the **SetFocus** method. In the current application, we want the focus to be put back on the combo box anytime a name is added or removed. As the program now stands, the focus stays on the command button requiring a user's move back to the combo box. Add the following line to *both* the **Met_Click()** and the **Oops_Click()** procedures:

Combo1.SetFocus

Insert this line right before the **End Sub** statement in each procedure to ensure that the focus goes to the combo box after a command button does its job.

Put It to Work

Run the program again and add names. As you type a name and press **Alt+M** or click the **Met** button, VB adds the name to the list, and the focus goes right back to the combo box, where you can immediately add another name. Now, display the combo box's list and highlight a name you want to remove. **Alt+O** removes the name and also moves the focus back to the combo box. Quit the application when you're through.

The Other Combo Box

Are you tired of the combo box's list closing as soon as you're done with it? When programmers first learn about combo boxes, they often fall into the trap of thinking that Visual Basic shouldn't close the combo box after each use. Keep in mind that a combo box's *primary benefit* is that it saves screen space. If you want a list continually displayed, use a list box.

If you use a simple combo box, you cannot close the box to a single line as you can with a drop-down combo box.

The second style of combo box, the simple combo style, gives you some of the advantages of the combo box you just used and of list boxes. You can see more of the list of items in the combo box, at the loss of some screen space.

Click the form's combo box (assuming that you've quit the application's execution) and press **F4** to display the Properties window. Change the Style properties to **1—Simple Combo**. Also, change the size of the combo box (you couldn't change this with the drop-down combo). Change the Height property to **1020**. The Height property is the only property you need to change.

Unlike the drop-down combo box you just used, you can adjust the size of a simple combo box so that more items in the list continually display at all times.

Run the program and see the difference. Follow these steps:

1. Enter **Lassie** and press **Alt+M**. Immediately, Visual Basic puts **Lassie** in the list.

2. Enter two more names—**Rover** and **Benji**—in the same way.

3. The combo box will not increase in size when you add a fourth name. Instead, Visual Basic displays a scroll bar. Add one more name, **Scruffy**, and as soon as you press **Alt+M**, you'll see scroll bars that you can click to scroll through the entire list. Figure 27.4 shows how your screen should look. That combo box is a pretty good control, huh?

Save your FAMOUS.MAK application so it will be ready to alter in Chapter 28, "Spicy Graphics." Save the form as FAMOUS.FRM if VB prompts you to do so.

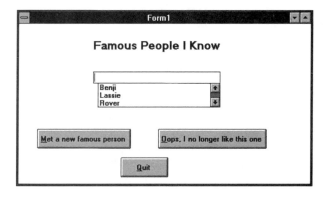

Figure 27.4

A simple combo box shows more stuff!

The Least You Need to Know

The two kinds of combo boxes give you a control that saves screen space over a list box, but still give you access to all items in the list. To add items to a combo box, you must use the **AddItem** method. The **RemoveItem** method deletes combo box items. Be sure to move the focus back to the combo box if you want to speed up the user's data entry. Here's what you learned in this chapter:

☛ A combo box takes less room than a list box. The choice depends on how much room your form has free.

☛ The two most common combo boxes are the drop-down combo box and the simple combo box.

☛ The drop-down combo box displays its list only when the user requests the display. The simple combo box always shows a few items in the list. The number of items shown is determined by the drop-down combo box's Height property.

☛ Use **AddItem** to add items to a combo box, **RemoveItem** to remove items from a combo box, and **SetFocus** to move the focus back to a combo box.

Part VI
A Taste of Your VB Future

Yikes! This book is coming to an end, and we've only scratched the surface of Visual Basic! That's okay though, because you're doing great. Now that you've mastered the fundamentals, everything else is a snap.

This last part of the book simply whets your appetite. I hope your imagined idiocy is coming to a screeching halt. As you've seen, Visual Basic is powerful and seems like a difficult program at first, but there's little to it when you tackle the basics.

Virtually everything else you'll learn as you grow your VB programming skills is little more than manipulating new controls in the same way as the ones that you know. A mouse click here and there and a mouse drag or two, and you've got a finished application faster than a C++ programmer can say "I'm ready to write a Windows program now."

Chapter 28
Spicy Graphics

In This Chapter

- ☛ Draw lines, circles, and squares!
- ☛ Modify the default Graphic controls' properties
- ☛ Use **LoadPicture()** to embed graphic images in your applications from outside picture files

So, you want to pretty up your applications? Today's computers provide support for graphics that were unheard of less than a decade ago. A computer program without graphics is like a day without sunshine. No Windows program is purely textual. Sure, a simple Windows-based word processor might deal exclusively in text, but the command buttons, scroll bars, and drop-down lists add a sharp edge to the textual nature, making the user feel as if she or he is working in front of a futuristic control panel instead of a 2-D computer screen.

This chapter gives you some insight into adding graphics to your programs. Just by selecting a Graphic control, you can draw lines, circles, and boxes on your screen to spruce up the look of your application.

Start Easy: The Line Control

The Line control is one of the easiest ways to add limited graphics to your application. The Line control draws a line on your form in any direction and for any length. (The Line control appears on the toolbox as a straight diagonal line.)

Here's a way to add a simple arrow pointing to the data-entry portion of a combo box:

1. Load the famous people application from the previous chapter if it's not currently loaded. Display the Form window by clicking the View Form command button in the Project window.

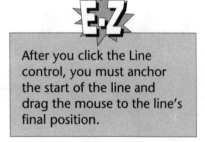

After you click the Line control, you must anchor the start of the line and drag the mouse to the line's final position.

2. Click the Line control.

3. Point to the left-hand side of the combo box's thin data-entry display window (where you enter names). About 0.5 inch to the left of the box, press the mouse button to anchor the start of the line.

4. Drag the mouse to the left, keeping the emerging line straight, until you see a straight line about 1 inch long. Let up on the mouse.

Click on the form anywhere within its white interior to set the straight line in place and to remove the two resizing handles. Your screen will look something like the one in Figure 28.1.

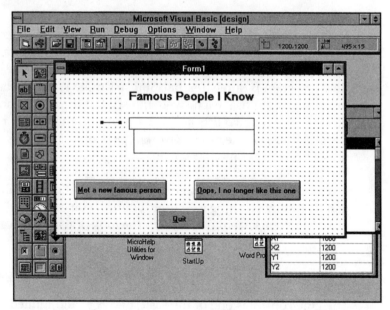

Figure 28.1

After drawing the body of an arrow.

5. Draw the point of the arrow using two diagonal straight lines beginning at the right end of the straight line.

6. Press **F5** to see the results. The arrow pointing to the data-entry part of the combo box helps the user find the data-entry section.

Both the Line control and the Shape control that you'll see next have many properties you can change. If you want a thicker line, change the BorderWidth to a value larger than 1. The BorderStyle gives you all kinds of lines from which to choose (for example, a dotted line). The BorderColor gives you an opportunity to draw colored lines.

More Than Boring Lines

The Shape control gives you many additional kinds of graphics. Figure 28.2 shows where the Shape control is located on the toolbox. (In the Standard Edition, the Shape control is the fourth tool from the bottom in the first column.) As with the other controls, you only have to click the Shape control and place the control on your Form window. However, unlike many of the other controls, the Shape control takes on many different personalities.

Shape control —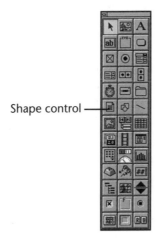

Figure 28.2

The Shape control draws pretty shapes.

If you choose the Shape control and place the shape on your form, Visual Basic begins with a squared rectangle.

The Shape control can draw any of the following shapes:

☞ Rectangles (and squares) with square corners

☞ Rectangles (and squares) with rounded corners

☞ Ovals

☞ Circles

Add a face to the FAMOUS.MAK application to give the user someone to look at.

1. Click the Shape control and place a large square to the right of the title label, as shown in Figure 28.3. Notice that the shape is a small square.

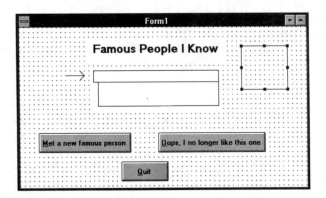

Figure 28.3

After placing the shape.

2. Press **F4** to display the Shape control's Properties window. Change the Shape property to **3—Circle**. As soon as you do, Visual Basic displays a circle inside the square shape.

3. Double-click the Shape control to place a large shape in the middle of the screen. Yikes, the shape is overwriting important stuff! Press **F4** and change the following properties to the values listed:

FillStyle: **0—Solid**
Height: **135**
Left: **6120**

Shape: **2—Oval**
Top: **1200**
Width: **495**

4. Place two more Shape controls like you did in Step 3. They should have the following properties:

FillStyle: **0—Solid**
Height: **135**
Left: **6120**
Shape: **0—Rectangle**
Top: **840**
Width: **135**

FillStyle: **0—Solid**
Height: **135**
Left: **6480**
Shape: **0—Rectangle**
Top: **840**
Width: **135**

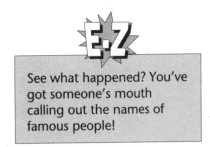

See what happened? You've got someone's mouth calling out the names of famous people!

Run the program, and you'll see the face, as shown in Figure 28.4.

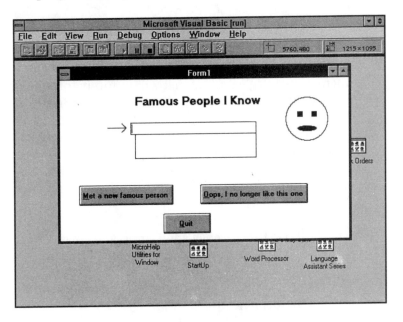

Figure 28.4

A face that calls out the names!

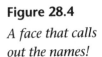

For practice, why don't you change the FillColor of the face's circle shape?

5. Save the program as FAMOUS.MAK and give your paintbrushes a rest.

Load Pictures!

Not only can you draw simple shapes, but you can also load icon files, bitmaps, and other common graphics files from the disk directly into your application. To display such a graphic file, you must use the Picture Box control located at the top of the toolbox's second column. The Picture Box control is the control with a sun shining down on the desert.

When you place a picture box, you don't actually place a graphic image but you place the *location* of a graphic image. To display and change pictures that appear inside the picture box, you'll usually use the **LoadPicture()** function inside the code window.

Most Windows picture files have the filename extensions .PCX, .BMP, .ICO, or .TIF.

Microsoft supplies lots of picture files with Visual Basic. There is a set of international flag icon files that will fit nicely into the international currency conversion program you wrote earlier in the book.

To change the currency conversion program so that the appropriate country's flag displays when the user clicks a non-U.S. currency, you'll have to add some code to the **List1_Click()** procedure. **List1_Click()** executes any time the user selects a non-U.S. currency from the list box. Follow these steps:

1. Load the currency application you created earlier.

2. Double-click the Picture Box control on the toolbox. Change the following properties:

   BorderStyle: **0—None**

Height: **495**
Left: **5400**
Top: **720**
Width: **495**

Notice that the name of the picture box is **Picture1** and that the Picture property is set to **(none)**, which means that no picture is loaded in the box at this time. Your code will perform the needed picture loading.

3. Double-click the list box to display the LIST1_Click () code.

4. At the end of the **Case "Italian Lira":** section (right before the second **Case** statement), add this line:

Picture1.Picture =
LoadPicture("c:\VB\icons\flags\flgitaly.ico")

When the user selects **Italian Lira**, not only does the conversion take place, but the **LoadPicture()** function also loads the Italian flag from the directory where Visual Basic stored the flag's pictures!

If your copy of Visual Basic is installed on a disk drive other than C:, change the **c:** to **d:** or whatever disk drive contains Visual Basic.

5. Finish loading the remaining flags by adding additional **Picture1.Picture** assignments for each currency. Here is the complete **List1_Click()** subroutine:

```
Sub List1_Click ()
  Select Case List1.Text
    Case "Italian Lira":
      ' Convert the US amount to Italian Lira
      ConvAmt.Caption = 2615 * USAmt.Text
      Picture1.Picture =
LoadPicture("c:\VB\icons\flags\flgitaly.ico")
    Case "French Franc":
      ' Convert the US amount to French Francs
      ConvAmt.Caption = 11.8 * USAmt.Text
      Picture1.Picture =
LoadPicture("c:\VB\icons\flags\flgfran.ico")
    Case "British Pound":
```

```
' Convert the US amount to British Pounds
ConvAmt.Caption = .75 * USAmt.Text
        Picture1.Picture =
LoadPicture("c:\VB\icons\flags\flguk.ico")
        Case "German Mark":
        ' Convert the US amount to German Marks
        ConvAmt.Caption = 4 * USAmt.Text
        Picture1.Picture =
LoadPicture("c:\VB\icons\flags\flggerm.ico")
        Case "Hong Kong Dollar":
        ' Convert the US amount to Hong Kong
Dollars
        ConvAmt.Caption = .18 * USAmt.Text
    Picture1.Picture =
LoadPicture("c:\VB\icons\flags\flguk.ico")
    End Select
End Sub
```

OOPS!

Visual Basic didn't supply a flag file for Hong Kong. The British flag is used here because of the control that Britain still has over Hong Kong until 1997. After 1997, the flag will change, and it's not yet determined exactly what that flag will be (although it probably will be the Chinese flag).

6. Run the program and click on a non-U.S. currency. Yeah! You see a flag pop up, like the one shown in Figure 28.5.

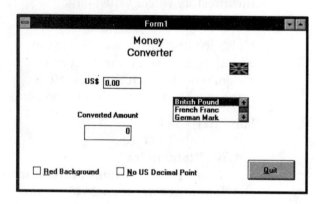

Figure 28.5

Displaying a flag for the currency.

The Least You Need to Know

You've now at least scratched the surface of Visual Basic's ability to add graphics to any program. There's a lot ahead of you, and as you advance your programming skills, you'll learn how Visual Basic supports animation and how you can add shapes to a form using just the Visual Basic programming language, without utilizing any controls. Such material is simply too advanced for this book because you've got to become more accustomed to the Visual Basic programming language before diving into such intricacies. Besides, many people program in Visual Basic for years and never need to master anything more than the Line, Shape, and Picture Box controls taught in this chapter because of the power these controls provide. Here's what you've learned in this chapter:

- Use the Line control to draw lines in any direction.

- The Shape control supports six different shapes: circles, ovals, rectangles with rounded corners, rectangles with square corners, squares with rounded corners, and squares with square corners.

- You can add graphics to your application from graphics files using the **LoadPicture()** function, as long as you first place a Picture Box control where the graphic will lie.

**This page requires the Alpha Books
Secret Decoder/Mood Ring (available at
fine stores everywhere in Upper Volta).**

Chapter 29

So, You Want to Use Disk Files?

In This Chapter

- ☛ The File-system controls eliminate long pathnames
- ☛ The three File-system controls handle disk drives, directories, and filenames
- ☛ Keep the File-system controls in synchronization with each other

This chapter explores some of VB's ability to get at files. Here, you'll find only an overview; complete books have been written on file access! Therefore, be warned that this material is more descriptive than instructive. Follow along with the examples, and you'll get a glimpse into Visual Basic's file access system that lets you perform file I/O.

I/O stands for *input/output*. Input/output is the name given to retrieving and saving data from and to your computer's devices, such as disk drives and modems.

The Standard File-System Controls

BY THE WAY

Figure 29.1 shows not *one* Visual Basic control, but a collection of *three*. You'll have to keep track of information in them all to find a certain file. In pre-Windows days, users had to type long pathnames, such as **c:\myapps\wordproc\sales.doc.** Now, users select from a dialog box, such as the one in Figure 29.1.

Figure 29.1 contains a familiar Windows dialog box. Whenever you open, save, or close files in Windows, you'll invariably see this dialog box, showing the following three pieces of information:

- ☞ A list of files
- ☞ A selected disk drive
- ☞ A list of directories

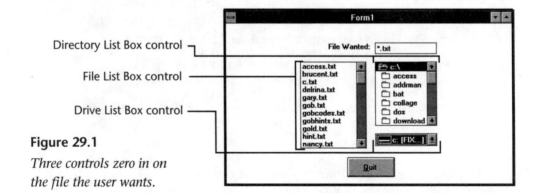

Directory List Box control ⌐

File List Box control ───

Drive List Box control ───

Figure 29.1

Three controls zero in on the file the user wants.

A regular Text Box control appears to the right of the **File Wanted:** label in Figure 29.1. To access the three File-system controls, you'll have to use the toolbox as usual: Click the control that you want and then size and place the control on the form.

Figure 29.2 shows where the three File-system controls appear on the toolbox.

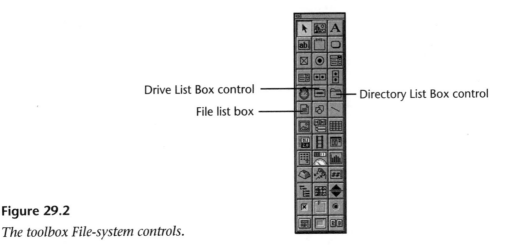

Drive List Box control —————— Directory List Box control

File list box ——————

Figure 29.2

The toolbox File-system controls.

Synchronizing the Controls

In creating the simple application shown in Figure 29.1, you'll get an idea of what's in store as you develop your file control abilities. Perhaps walking through this example will raise more questions than it answers, but the most important thing you'll gain is a knowledge of how you tie together the File-system controls. In other words, if the user chooses a different disk drive, you'll have to make sure that the file list changes as well as the directory list.

To keep things easy, this application simply manipulates the File-system controls. You won't actually *see* the contents of any files—that's your homework project once you finish this book.

Open a new project and place the controls as follows:

1. Place a Label control on the form, with the following properties:

   Alignment: **1—Right Justify**
   Caption: **File Wanted:**
   Height: **255**
   Left: **2400**
   Top: **480**
   Width: **1335**

BY THE WAY

The Text property describes the files shown when the application starts up (all files that end with the .TXT extension).

2. Place a Text Box control on the form, with the following properties:

   Height: **285**
   Left: **3840**
   TabIndex: **1**
   Text: ***.TXT**
   Top: **480**
   Width: **1575**

3. Place a File List Box control on the form, with the following properties:

   Height: **2175**
   Left: **1920**
   Pattern: ***.TXT**
   Top: **960**
   Width: **1695**

4. Place a Directory List Box control on the form, with the following properties:

   Height: **1605**
   Left: **3840**
   Top: **960**
   Width: **1575**

5. Place a Drive List Box control on the form, with the following properties:

   Height: **315**
   Left: **3840**
   Top: **2760**
   Width: **1575**

6. Finally, put a **&Quit** command button at the bottom of the form. Add the **End** statement to the command button's **Click** procedure, as you've done throughout this book.

The Start-Up Code

When you run the program, the first thing you want to do is set the screen's controls to display a specific path. If you do not specify a pathname, the controls will often show the last path accessed by a Windows program.

Unless you need to zero in on a different directory, drive C's root directory, specified by **c:**, is usually the best default directory to begin any file listing with.

The **Form_Load()** subroutine sets up the application so that the correct path first appears. Double-click on the form's background and add the following **Form_Load()** subroutine in the code window:

```
Sub Form_Load ()
   Drive1.Drive = "c:"
   Dir1.Path = "c:\"
End Sub
```

In Sync

The only thing left to do is tie everything together so that when the user changes a drive, pathname, or **File Wanted** description, the other File-system controls update as well.

The Drive list box (named **Drive1**) Drive property determines the disk drive name displayed. The Directory list box (named **Dir1**) Path property determines the pathname displayed.

Double-click the text box (the control to the right of **File Wanted:**). Add to the code body so that **Text1_Change()** looks like this:

```
Sub Text1_Change ()
   File1.Pattern = Text1.Text
End Sub
```

Changing the **File1** control (the File List Box control) forces the file list in the **File1** File list box to change.

TECHNO NERD TEACHES...

Often, when one event's subroutine changes a control, a second subroutine executes. Suppose that you write a **ControlName_Change()** subroutine that executes whenever the user changes the control named **ControlName**. If another subroutine modifies **ControlName**'s value, as opposed to the user changing the value, the **ControlName_Change()** subroutine executes if that subroutine contains code.

In other words, **ControlName_Change()** executes any time the control named **ControlName** changes, whether those changes are made by the user or by another subroutine. Knowing this provides the framework for the File-system controls. When the user enters a new disk drive in the Drive list box, that Drive list box's **Change()** subroutine must trigger other file-system **Change()** routines so that their values update to reflect the change.

You must now make sure that when the user changes the disk drive, the file list, *as well as* the directory list, changes. Therefore, double-click the Drive List control and add to the code body so that the **Drive1_Change()** subroutine looks like this:

```
Sub Drive1_Change ()
   Dir1.Path = Drive1.Drive
End Sub
```

Changing the **Dir1**'s Path property forces an execution of the **Drive1_Change()** subroutine if you've coded such a subroutine. You'll want the file list to change if the directory ever changes, so close the code window and double-click the Directory list box. Add to the code body so that **Dir1_Change()** looks like this:

```
Sub Dir1_Change ()
   File1.Path = Dir1.Path
End Sub
```

You've now got a filename displayer that contains a set of File-system controls that work together. Run the program and change the default filename extension, change the disk drive, and change the directory, and you'll see that the File list properly updates to put the changes into effect.

Looking Ahead

There is a good reason that this chapter does not go ahead and show you the contents of a file chosen in the application: Files come in all sorts of formats. The least common denominator, text files, are the easiest to read but are the least-common type of file. (Of all the files on your hard disk, perhaps fewer than two percent are text files.)

A *text file* is an uncompressed file that holds... well...text. Virtually all programs read and write text files. Often, text files are called *ASCII files*.

Therefore, to view each individual file with this application would mean writing a different file-viewing routine for each type of file, and that's not only beyond the scope of this book but beyond the scope of most programmers!

Often, you don't want to see the contents of every file, especially executable files. Primarily, you'll want to write applications that input and output the user's data.

After a good rest from finishing this book, you'll be ready to begin looking into the fundamentals of data storage and retrieval. Chapter 30, "What's Next?" lists some good Visual Basic references that delve into file access.

The Least You Need to Know

The File-system controls work together to let your user select the appropriate disk drive, directory, and filename. A lot happens behind the scenes when you use the File-system controls, but you must make sure that changes occur in synchronization with each other. To do that, you must keep in mind the following:

- ☞ The File-system controls give your user drive, directory, and file-selection choices.

- ☞ When your application begins, you must set the default directory (usually to the root directory of C:).

- ☞ As you link together the File-system controls, change the file list *and* directory list when the disk drive changes, change the file list when the file extension changes, and change the file list when the directory list changes.

Chapter 30
What's Next?

In This Chapter

- ☞ Learn the advanced features of Visual Basic

- ☞ See how the Professional Edition supports more data formats

- ☞ Take note of other excellent Visual Basic references

Be proud! You're no Visual Basic idiot! Let's stress again that you are creating applications that used to take long and tedious hours to develop, using traditional Windows-based programming tools such as C and C++.

If you're wanting to look into the other controls that this book didn't get to, *go ahead*! You'll place them, resize them, and change their properties just as you've done now for 29 chapters. Click on a control, read its properties, and search the online help for reference to master that control's advantages.

Advanced Features

Although you should practice a bit with what you've learned, you might want to take a peek at other features of Visual Basic that lie in your

If you understand the fundamentals, you'll find nothing in Visual Basic that is difficult.

programming future. Before you do, understand that you don't have to memorize all the properties, controls, and Visual Basic language commands to use them. With this book, the online help, and a few mouse clicks on VB's windows, you can do virtually anything.

Here is a list of Visual Basic's most important features:

1. **The Microsoft Access database engine**

Microsoft Access is a powerful PC-based database program. Access includes a Visual Basic-like programming language; therefore, once you master Visual Basic, you'll have a firm foothold on the programming language of Access.

A *database* program tracks, inputs, processes, and outputs vast amounts of data using an organized structure and (often) a simple interface.

Although Access includes a VB-like language, Access does not replace Visual Basic. VB is a general-purpose Windows application development system, whereas Access is built around its database activities.

Visual Basic includes commands, functions, and controls that access (read, write, delete, and change) data created from within Access. Therefore, if you or others develop Access-based applications, you'll be able to interact with those Access databases much more easily than you can interact with other kinds of databases.

Visual Basic does read and write the following database file formats in addition to Access: FoxPro, dBASE, Paradox, and BTrieve files. Visual Basic does not support the fully optimized query and tracking features for these formats as it does for Access database files.

2. **OLE 1.0 and 2.0 support**

   If another application, such as Excel 5.0, supports OLE, your Visual Basic application will be able to manipulate that application's objects (such as spreadsheet cells, formats, and so forth).

   OLE stands for object linking and embedding.

   OLE is considered a programmer's nightmare. To make two different kinds of applications speak to each other requires a thorough knowledge of each application as well as the documented OLE protocols.

   Visual Basic is the first programming tool that has OLE functionality for the masses. With the OLE controls, a few simple clicks, drags, and property settings virtually finalize your VB program's interaction with other programs.

3. **Setup Wizard**

   If you distribute your VB applications to other users, those users will need an automated way to install and set up their programs. Starting with version 3.0, Visual Basic provides the Setup Wizard feature, which walks you through the creation of a user's installation to provide a uniform installation procedure for your users.

   The following features are available only for Professional Edition Visual Basic users.

4. **SQL and ODBC server**

   To make up for the various database formats not directly supported by Visual Basic, Microsoft added to VB an interface for databases that support the SQL and ODBC standards. SQL is a common database access language supported by many database vendors, and ODBC is a common set of routines that access data from databases in a consistent manner, no matter how that data is stored.

SQL stands for Structured Query Language and *ODCB* stands for Open Database Connectivity.

Do you get the idea that access to a large number of databases is significant? In today's world, information is a vital resource and the more kinds of data that VB can work with, the more likely companies are to adopt Visual Basic as their front-end system for users.

5. ***Crystal Reports* report writer**

The Professional Edition contains a *report writer* that adds customized professional-looking printed reports to your VB applications. After all, what is data access if you cannot print that data in an organized manner? Without the report writer, designing and coding printed reports from Visual Basic is tedious.

6. **Data-aware control development kit**

With the Professional Edition, you can create your own controls. If you want a special trio of push buttons, dials that move as data increases or shrinks, special clock controls, calendar controls, color-changing controls, or any other types of controls that your imagination comes up with, you can use the control development kit to create such controls.

A Head Start on VBA

Visual Basic for Applications, or *VBA* as Microsoft refers to it, is a Visual Basic–like programming language that Microsoft is planning to put in all its applications. The first two applications to utilize VBA are the

Microsoft Excel spreadsheet and the Microsoft Project project management system.

Whereas Access contains a Visual Basic–like language, Access does not provide support for the complete VBA as do the two applications just mentioned. Soon, however, all Microsoft products, from Word to Access, will include the same VBA programming language, and that language will be nothing more than Visual Basic. Each application will include its own set of specialized functions that take advantage of the specific application's requirements, but the underlying language will be Visual Basic.

These applications used to have a special limited language called a *macro language* that controlled the application. The macro languages were not only more limiting than Visual Basic, but they were different with each program. VBA promises to add a consistent programming language to every Microsoft application and any other vendor's application that supports VBA. (The applications still support the macro languages, but Microsoft encourages users not to use them.)

You've got a head start on VBA! Instead of learning a separate language for Excel, a separate language for Word, and so on, you already understand the fundamentals for controlling these languages!

Other Sources

The following books are excellent guides for extending your current Visual Basic knowledge, taking your beginning skills to newfound advanced territories:

Teach Yourself Visual Basic 3 in 21 Days

Database Developer's Guide with Visual Basic 3

Secrets of the Visual Basic 3 Masters

Teach Yourself Visual Basic for Applications in 21 Days

Some companies are finding their fortunes in selling custom controls. Visual Basic is responsible for growing this section of the data processing industry because of VB's use of controls. If you develop a neat control that you think others will want to use, you can package that control and give or sell the control to others who program with Visual Basic.

Dive In, the Water's Warm!

The three most important things you can do to expand your Visual Basic skills are

- ☞ Practice

- ☞ Practice

- ☞ Practice

Make up simple applications, try different controls, make mistakes, correct the mistakes, and above all else, have fun with Visual Basic. Only then will you move to the programming ranks of *VB guru*.

Appendix A
ASCII Table

Dec X_{10}	Hex X_{16}	Binary X_2	ASCII Character
000	00	0000 0000	null
001	01	0000 0001	☺
002	02	0000 0010	☻
003	03	0000 0011	♥
004	04	0000 0100	◆
005	05	0000 0101	♣
006	06	0000 0110	♠
007	07	0000 0111	●
008	08	0000 1000	■
009	09	0000 1001	○
010	0A	0000 1010	■
011	0B	0000 1011	♂
012	0C	0000 1100	♀
013	0D	0000 1101	♪
014	0E	0000 1110	♪♪
015	0F	0000 1111	☼
016	10	0001 0000	►
017	11	0001 0001	◄
018	12	0001 0010	↕
019	13	0001 0011	‼
020	14	0001 0100	¶
021	15	0001 0101	§
022	16	0001 0110	−
023	17	0001 0111	↨

Dec X_{10}	Hex X_{16}	Binary X_2	ASCII Character
024	18	0001 1000	↑
025	19	0001 1001	↓
026	1A	0001 1010	→
027	1B	0001 1011	←
028	1C	0001 1100	FS
029	1D	0001 1101	GS
030	1E	0001 1110	RS
031	1F	0001 1111	US
032	20	0010 0000	SP
033	21	0010 0001	!
034	22	0010 0010	"
035	23	0010 0011	#
036	24	0010 0100	$
037	25	0010 0101	%
038	26	0010 0110	&
039	27	0010 0111	'
040	28	0010 1000	(
041	29	0010 1001	)
042	2A	0010 1010	*
043	2B	0010 1011	+
044	2C	0010 1100	'
045	2D	0010 1101	-
046	2E	0010 1110	.
047	2F	0010 1111	/
048	30	0011 0000	0
049	31	0011 0001	1
050	32	0011 0010	2
051	33	0011 0011	3
052	34	0011 0100	4
053	35	0011 0101	5
054	36	0011 0110	6

Dec X_{10}	Hex X_{16}	Binary X_2	ASCII Character
055	37	0011 0111	7
056	38	0011 1000	8
057	39	0011 1001	9
058	3A	0011 1010	:
059	3B	0011 1011	;
060	3C	0011 1100	<
061	3D	0011 1101	=
062	3E	0011 1110	>
063	3F	0011 1111	?
064	40	0100 0000	@
065	41	0100 0001	A
066	42	0100 0010	B
067	43	0100 0011	C
068	44	0100 0100	D
069	45	0100 0101	E
070	46	0100 0110	F
071	47	0100 0111	G
072	48	0100 1000	H
073	49	0100 1001	I
074	4A	0100 1010	J
075	4B	0100 1011	K
076	4C	0100 1100	L
077	4D	0100 1101	M
078	4E	0100 1110	N
079	4F	0100 1111	O
080	50	0101 0000	P
081	51	0101 0001	Q
082	52	0101 0010	R
083	53	0101 0011	S
084	54	0101 0100	T
085	55	0101 0101	U

Dec X_{10}	Hex X_{16}	Binary X_2	ASCII Character
086	56	0101 0110	V
087	57	0101 0111	W
088	58	0101 1000	X
089	59	0101 1001	Y
090	5A	0101 1010	Z
091	5B	0101 1011	[
092	5C	0101 1100	\
093	5D	0101 1101	]
094	5E	0101 1110	^
095	5F	0101 1111	–
096	60	0110 0000	`
097	61	0110 0001	a
098	62	0110 0010	b
099	63	0110 0011	c
100	64	0110 0100	d
101	65	0110 0101	e
102	66	0110 0110	f
103	67	0110 0111	g
104	68	0110 1000	h
105	69	0110 1001	i
106	6A	0110 1010	j
107	6B	0110 1011	k
108	6C	0110 1100	l
109	6D	0110 1101	m
110	6E	0110 1110	n
111	6F	0110 1111	o
112	70	0111 0000	p
113	71	0111 0001	q
114	72	0111 0010	r
115	73	0111 0011	s
116	74	0111 0100	t
117	75	0111 0101	u
118	76	0111 0110	v
119	77	0111 0111	w

Dec X_{10}	Hex X_{16}	Binary X_2	ASCII Character
120	78	0111 1000	x
121	79	0111 1001	y
122	7A	0111 1010	z
123	7B	0111 1011	{
124	7C	0111 1100	¦
125	7D	0111 1101	}
126	7E	0111 1110	~
127	7F	0111 1111	DEL
128	80	1000 0000	Ç
129	81	1000 0001	ü
130	82	1000 0010	é
131	83	1000 0011	â
132	84	1000 0100	ä
133	85	1000 0101	à
134	86	1000 0110	å
135	87	1000 0111	ç
136	88	1000 1000	ê
137	89	1000 1001	ë
138	8A	1000 1010	è
139	8B	1000 1011	ï
140	8C	1000 1100	î
141	8D	1000 1101	ì
142	8E	1000 1110	Ä
143	8F	1000 1111	Å
144	90	1001 0000	É
145	91	1001 0001	æ
146	92	1001 0010	Æ
147	93	1001 0011	ô
148	94	1001 0100	ö
149	95	1001 0101	ò
150	96	1001 0110	û
151	97	1001 0111	ù
152	98	1001 1000	ÿ
153	99	1001 1001	Ö

Dec X_{10}	Hex X_{16}	Binary X_2	ASCII Character
154	9A	1001 1010	Ü
155	9B	1001 1011	¢
156	9C	1001 1100	£
157	9D	1001 1101	¥
158	9E	1001 1110	Pt
159	9F	1001 1111	*f*
160	A0	1010 0000	á
161	A1	1010 0001	í
162	A2	1010 0010	ó
163	A3	1010 0011	ú
164	A4	1010 0100	ñ
165	A5	1010 0101	Ñ
166	A6	1010 0110	a
167	A7	1010 0111	o
168	A8	1010 1000	¿
169	A9	1010 1001	⌐
170	AA	1010 1010	¬
171	AB	1010 1011	½
172	AC	1010 1100	¼
173	AD	1010 1101	¡
174	AE	1010 1110	«
175	AF	1010 1111	»
176	B0	1011 0000	▒
177	B1	1011 0001	▓
178	B2	1011 0010	█
179	B3	1011 0011	│
180	B4	1011 0100	┤
181	B5	1011 0101	╡
182	B6	1011 0110	╢
183	B7	1011 0111	╖
184	B8	1011 1000	╕
185	B9	1011 1001	╣
186	BA	1011 1010	║
187	BB	1011 1011	╗

Dec X_{10}	Hex X_{16}	Binary X_2	ASCII Character
188	BC	1011 1100	⌐
189	BD	1011 1101	⊔
190	BE	1011 1110	⌐
191	BF	1011 1111	¬
192	C0	1100 0000	└
193	C1	1100 0001	⊥
194	C2	1100 0010	⊤
195	C3	1100 0011	├
196	C4	1100 0100	—
197	C5	1100 0101	+
198	C6	1100 0110	
199	C7	1100 0111	╟
200	C8	1100 1000	╚
201	C9	1100 1001	╔
202	CA	1100 1010	╩
203	CB	1100 1011	╦
204	CC	1100 1100	╠
205	CD	1100 1101	=
206	CE	1100 1110	╬
207	CF	1100 1111	╧
208	D0	1101 0000	╨
209	D1	1101 0001	╤
210	D2	1101 0010	╥
211	D3	1101 0011	╙
212	D4	1101 0100	╘
213	D5	1101 0101	╒
214	D6	1101 0110	╓
215	D7	1101 0111	╫
216	D8	1101 1000	╪
217	D9	1101 1001	┘
218	DA	1101 1010	┌
219	DB	1101 1011	█
220	DC	1101 1100	▄
221	DD	1101 1101	▌

Dec X_{10}	Hex X_{16}	Binary X_2	ASCII Character
222	DE	1101 1110	▮
223	DF	1101 1111	▪
224	E0	1110 0000	α
225	E1	1110 0001	β
226	E2	1110 0010	Γ
227	E3	1110 0011	π
228	E4	1110 0100	Σ
229	E5	1110 0101	σ
230	E6	1110 0110	μ
231	E7	1110 0111	τ
232	E8	1110 1000	Φ
233	E9	1110 1001	θ
234	EA	1110 1010	Ω
235	EB	1110 1011	δ
236	EC	1110 1100	∞
237	ED	1110 1101	ø
238	EE	1110 1110	∈
239	EF	1110 1111	∩
240	F0	1110 0000	≡
241	F1	1111 0001	±
242	F2	1111 0010	≥
243	F3	1111 0011	≤
244	F4	1111 0100	⌠
245	F5	1111 0101	⌡
246	F6	1111 0110	÷
247	F7	1111 0111	≈
248	F8	1111 1000	°
249	F9	1111 1001	•
250	FA	1111 1010	·
251	FB	1111 1011	√
252	FC	1111 1100	η
253	FD	1111 1101	2
254	FE	1111 1110	▪
255	FF	1111 1111	

Glossary
Speak Like a Geek: The Complete Archive

This glossary contains, in alphabetical order, all the special terms that were defined in the book.

accelerator keys   Shortcut keys that speed your menu selections.

application   Computer lingo for programs that you and others write.

ASCII table   Assigns a numeric, coded value to every possible character your PC can produce. (See Appendix A, "ASCII Table," for an ASCII table.)

assignment statement   Assigns values to properties and variables.

BASIC   An acronym that stands for *Beginner's All-Purpose Symbolic Instruction Code.*

bug   A mistake that you or somebody else puts into a program.

calling   This describes the action that occurs when one subroutine triggers the execution of another.

code   A bunch of close-but-not-English Visual Basic commands that you sometimes type.

command button   A control that lets your user signal that he or she is ready to proceed with an action of some kind.

concatenation A silver dollar word that means stringing one chunk of text together with another chunk of text to form a single, longer chunk of text.

context-sensitive help This is the name for the help awareness that enables VB to look at what you're currently doing and display help on that topic.

controls For some reason, Microsoft insists on calling the toolbox items controls instead of tools. Much of the time, this book does also, just to make Microsoft happy. Controls are buttons, dials, and other tools that give your users the ability to manage a running program.

decremented variable A variable from which *n* has been subtracted.

dialog box A control that resembles a small window. Users can enter data into applications through Dialog Box controls.

function A lot like a subroutine in that it's a small section of code that executes when a certain event happens. For now, you can consider a function and subroutine to be the same thing.

incremented variable A variable to which *n* has been added.

input Any data, keystrokes, or mouse movements sent to your program, as opposed to *output*, which is data you see on the screen or printer, or data sent to a disk file from your program.

input boxes Pop-up boxes that appear on the screen when input is needed.

iteration A single execution of a loop's body of code. If the body of a loop executes three times, three iterations are said to have occurred.

justification Describes text. When left-justified, text appears against the left side of a control. When right-justified, the text appears against the right side of a control. When centered, the text sits right in the middle of a control.

message boxes Pop-up boxes that appear on the screen when message output is needed.

mutually exclusive options   Only one of these can be selected at any one time.

nested loop   One loop inside another loop.

online   On the disk and ready for you to call up at any time.

operator   A symbol, such as the plus sign, that does mathematic work.

procedure   A general name for both functions and subroutines.

project   A collection of VB routines, screen controls, forms, code, and everything else that makes up a Visual Basic application.

property   A characteristic or behavior of a control, form, or other VB element.

prototype   A working model of something. C and C++ programmers create prototypes in Visual Basic before using C and C++.

read-only property   A property that is fixed and that you cannot change.

reserved word (or keyword)   A VB command, such as **End** or **Sub**.

resizing handles   The eight little black squares around the command button.

returns   The action taken by a function when the function finishes executing and sends (returns) the program control back to the calling code.

scroll bars   Controls that look like elevator shafts and give users the ability to pan through a list of choices or text.

string   A computer term for zero or more characters (letters, digits, or special characters such as *, &, and $) strung together and taken as a whole chunk; for example, a name, address, or city name.

syntax   A language's spelling and grammar rules.

text editor   Similar to a simple word processor.

text file   An uncompressed file that holds text. Virtually all programs can read and write text files.

truncate   To chop off and remove.

twip   1/4400 of an inch (very small indeed); used for Windows screen measurements.

users   People who use programs.

variable   A named storage place in memory.

Index

Who cares what you think? WE DO!

We take our customers' opinions very personally. After all, you're the reason we publish these books. If you're not happy, we're doing something wrong.

We'd appreciate it if you would take the time to drop us a note or fax us a fax. A real person—not a computer—reads every letter we get, and makes sure that your comments get relayed to the appropriate people.

Not sure what to say? Here are some details we'd like to know:

- ☞ Who you are (age, occupation, hobbies, etc.)
- ☞ Where you bought the book
- ☞ Why you picked this book instead of a different one
- ☞ What you liked best about the book
- ☞ What could have been done better
- ☞ Your overall opinion of the book
- ☞ What other topics you would purchase a book on

Mail, e-mail, or fax it to:

Faithe Wempen
Product Development Manager
Alpha Books
201 West 103rd Street
Indianapolis, IN 46290

FAX: (317) 581-4669
CIS: 75430,174

Special Offer!

Alpha Books needs people like you to give opinions about new and existing books. Product testers receive free books in exchange for providing their opinions about them. If you would like to be a product tester, please mention it in your letter, and make sure you include your full name, address, and daytime phone.

GO AHEAD. PLUG YOURSELF INTO
PRENTICE HALL COMPUTER PUBLISHING.

Introducing the PHCP Forum on CompuServe®

Yes, it's true. Now, you can have CompuServe access to the same professional, friendly folks who have made computers easier for years. On the PHCP Forum, you'll find additional information on the topics covered by every PHCP imprint—including Que, Sams Publishing, New Riders Publishing, Alpha Books, Brady Books, Hayden Books, and Adobe Press. In addition, you'll be able to receive technical support and disk updates for the software produced by Que Software and Paramount Interactive, a division of the Paramount Technology Group. It's a great way to supplement the best information in the business.

WHAT CAN YOU DO ON THE PHCP FORUM?

Play an important role in the publishing process—and make our books better while you make your work easier:

- Leave messages and ask questions about PHCP books and software—you're guaranteed a response within 24 hours
- Download helpful tips and software to help you get the most out of your computer
- Contact authors of your favorite PHCP books through electronic mail
- Present your own book ideas
- Keep up to date on all the latest books available from each of PHCP's exciting imprints

JOIN NOW AND GET A FREE COMPUSERVE STARTER KIT!

To receive your free CompuServe Introductory Membership, call toll-free, **1-800-848-8199** and ask for representative **#597**. The Starter Kit Includes:

- Personal ID number and password
- $15 credit on the system
- Subscription to CompuServe Magazine

HERE'S HOW TO PLUG INTO PHCP:

Once on the CompuServe System, type any of these phrases to access the PHCP Forum:

GO PHCP   **GO BRADY**
GO QUEBOOKS   **GO HAYDEN**
GO SAMS   **GO QUESOFT**
GO NEWRIDERS   **GO PARAMOUNTINTER**
GO ALPHA

Once you're on the CompuServe Information Service, be sure to take advantage of all of CompuServe's resources. CompuServe is home to more than 1,700 products and services—plus it has over 1.5 million members worldwide. You'll find valuable online reference materials, travel and investor services, electronic mail, weather updates, leisure-time games and hassle-free shopping (no jam-packed parking lots or crowded stores).

Seek out the hundreds of other forums that populate CompuServe. Covering diverse topics such as pet care, rock music, cooking, and political issues, you're sure to find others with the sames concerns as you—and expand your knowledge at the same time.